SAFE
Tennis

SAFE
Tennis

*How to Train and Play to Avoid
Injury and Stay Healthy*

By Jim Martz

Foreword by Nick Bollettieri

Skyhorse Publishing books may be purchased in bulk at special discounts for sales promotion, corporate gifts, fund-raising, or educational purposes. Special editions can also be created to specifications. For details, contact the Special Sales Department, Skyhorse Publishing, 307 West 36th Street, 11th Floor, New York, NY 10018 or info@skyhorsepublishing.com.

Skyhorse® and Skyhorse Publishing® are registered trademarks of Skyhorse Publishing, Inc.®, a Delaware corporation.

Visit our website at www.skyhorsepublishing.com.

10 9 8 7 6 5 4 3 2 1

Library of Congress Cataloging-in-Publication Data is available on file.

Interior photos by Al Messerschmidt

Cover design by Jane Shepard
Cover photo credit Thinkstock

ISBN: 978-1-63220-496-7
Ebook ISBN 978-1-63220-856-9

Printed in the United States of America

CONTENTS

FOREWORD

Sports injuries can be both debilitating and career-ending. Modern-day athletes, even the weekend type, are beginning to appreciate the importance of preparing before competing. The old saying: "Failing to plan is planning to fail" is true in every field of endeavor.

I first started teaching tennis in the late 1950s at Victory Park in North Miami Beach, Florida. My students would come for their lesson and, from the very first strike of the ball, crushed the ball with all their might. Imagine if I had insisted that they first do 15 minutes of stretching exercises and rope-skipping to protect them from injury. Even though I was charging only $3.00 per hour, parents would have demanded a refund.

Modern-day athletes, both professional and amateur, realize the importance of remaining injury-free. Professional athletes now have teams that include specialists in technique, as well as physical and mental conditioning. While the average weekend athlete doesn't need, nor could she/he afford to employ such a team of specialists, it is important to understand that injuries don't only affect your performance on the court. They affect family, recreation, and job performance.

The most common sports injuries are strains and sprains. These injuries are the result of the sudden stretching of ligaments beyond their limits. Sometimes the prevention of common injuries is beyond our control, but in many cases, these injuries are preventable. Proper warm-up increases blood flow to your muscles and decreases the likelihood of over-stretching.

Professional athletes begin their training weeks before a major competition. How often have we heard boxers say that they have been in training camp for six weeks?

Weekend warriors, on the other hand, don't have that luxury. The wisest thing that they can do is to slowly warm up each of the muscle groups before playing. By the way, strains and sprains are also the most common injuries in children. Almost 500,000 children are diagnosed with these injuries each year. It is not unusual for children to begin learning tennis at the age of 5 or 6 years. Growth plate injuries are very common in children. When the growing process is complete, the growth plate is replaced by solid bone. So, be sure to monitor the amount of training or competing that you allow for young children. Again, the most sensible way to prevent all sports injuries is to teach kids to stretch and warm up before practices and matches. Kids often feel invincible. Make warm-up a regimen that they perform because they realize that rehabilitation is not fun and the time away from the game to rehabilitate an injury can be a major setback.

One other area of concern for the weekend warrior is fatigue. Fatigue removes all of your protective efforts. Once fatigued, your risk to primary and secondary injuries increases. So, know when to say, "I've had enough!" Try to be in the best shape you can, and fatigue won't set in as quickly. I can't tell you the number of times that I've continued to play after fatigue had set in. I didn't realize how vulnerable I was making myself to a muscle or ligament injury.

Develop a warm-up strategy before each physical activity and a cool-down strategy after each event. And stick to that regimen. It will probably help you remain injury-free and improve the quality of your life!

– Nick Bollettieri, Founder and President
Emeritus IMG Academy—Bollettieri Tennis Program;
International Tennis Hall of Fame Inductee 2014

INTRODUCTION: AVOIDING INJURIES IS A HEALTHY ACTIVITY FOR EVERYONE

When fitness expert Jeff Drock was asked how important it is to avoid those nagging tennis injuries that could wipe out a player's season, he quickly replied, "You want to keep them off the operating table."

He wasn't kidding. As he pointed out, every strength and conditioning coach's goal should be injury prevention.

Preparing the correct way is important in everything you do in life, but if you don't warm up properly before playing tennis you could end up in the hospital. Consider how often professional tennis players are undergoing injuries—especially to the shoulder and wrist—sometimes bringing a much-too-early finish to a promising career. And these are athletes in peak physical condition.

Therefore, imagine the risk you or your kids undertake when you venture out for your weekly tennis match.

Safe Tennis, with instructive images, teaches you how to avoid these injuries and how to properly prepare yourself. There are detailed warm-up plans and exercises that specifically strengthen you for a tennis match. This includes stretching exercises that are designed by physical therapists who specialize in sports medicine.

In addition, you will learn how to prevent injuries while on the court, learn the correct way to cool down after your match, and perform specific exercises if therapy is needed. There are tips on how to schedule your workouts, matches, rest time, and recovery, plus the mental aspect as it relates to injuries and fitness.

When sports psychologist John F. Murray, Ph.D., was asked about the importance of avoiding and coping with tennis injuries, he noted that avoiding injury and staying healthy fall within the area of well-being, and that we know from numerous studies that a sound and healthy mind or mental skills feed a sense of physical health and well-being. And when things are not going well physically, or an athlete is experiencing an injury, mental stability can often suffer.

As the late renowned coach, psychologist, and researcher Vic Braden noted, one must understand that the muscle has no memory, and so we have to focus on the human brain.

When Satoshi Ochi, the Head Strength and Conditioning Coach for the United States Tennis Association's High Performance facility in Florida, was asked about the importance of this topic, he replied, "Well, it's huge. Tennis players spend so much time on the tennis court in practice and getting better in their game. And at the same time you spend so much time on the fitness and conditioning and other areas. And if you don't treat your body right, all the work you've put on the body, you can't use it.

"At any level, you have to take care of your body. It's injury prevention. And tennis is such a complex movement, right and left, it is designed to create some imbalance in the body. It's important to work on injury prevention at the same time you train for tennis so that you won't put yourself in a situation in which you might get injured."

As renowned sports psychologist and author Jim Loehr, Ph.D., points out, tennis is a very demanding sport. You are all alone on the court (unless you're playing doubles), matches can go for hours, there are no timeouts, and the scoring system in tennis promotes mounting pressure.

"There are numerous ways for cheating," he adds, "and the sport can become expensive: Court time, tournament entry fees, racquets, balls, shoes, instruction, travel to tournaments, and rivalries can be bigger than life."

Rick Macci, a veteran teaching pro who coached five players in their formative years who eventually became number 1 in the world, offers this advice for parents: "You have to remember it's not one size fits all. What I mean by that, you can't have a blueprint of here's what you're supposed to do at five, seven, nine, ten [years old]. Kids come in all shapes and sizes with different height and weight. So that's going to really be the mitigating factor of what a child can and cannot do. So I think you've got to be careful or you're going down a slippery slope if they start, say, lifting weights at a certain age or doing too much of something at a certain age. I think you've really got to know your child and you need to have experts who have been around kids a lot and who have seen this, because there could be an eight-year-old who is way more developed than at twelve. And vice versa.

"So, you've got to be really careful. That would be the first thing that I would throw out to any parent because a lot are novices, or perhaps they haven't been down this road before and they just think more is better. They see what other people are doing or hear what other people are doing. But that's pretty much related to that child. There will be some commonalities according to age, but it's more based on talent than on the physical nature of the child."

Training to enhance performance and to prevent injury often go hand in hand for players of all levels, says E. Paul Roetert, who holds a Ph.D. in biomechanics, and Mark S. Kovacs, who has a Ph.D. in exercise physiology. Roetert for many years was the managing director of the USTA, and Kovacs served as the Senior Manager of Sports Science and Coaching Education for the USTA.

They note that injuries in tennis typically are minor, but they can and do occur. And they can be acute, such as ankle sprains or persistent shoulder pain. They believe much can be done to prevent injuries by designing and following a proper conditioning program as well as playing with equipment appropriate for your game.

Following the advice of these and other experts, you can curb your worry of nagging injuries, and your time on the court will be much more enjoyable.

The exercises in *Safe Tennis* are to be performed only under the supervision and guidance of a certified strength and conditioning specialist, or a very experienced tennis coaching professional. Any exercises depicted in the book are for demonstration purposes only. Your possession of this book is in no way a prescription of exercises and is only to be used as a guide.

COMMON INJURIES

U nless you are a physician or fitness trainer, you probably have not heard of humeral epicondylitis. But if you are a weekend hacker or just taking up the sport of tennis, you may have felt humeral epicondylitis. And you may have screeched.

Humeral epicondylitis goes by the more common name of tennis elbow. This is one of the most frequent injuries in the sport but usually affects recreational players, not professionals.

In the book *It Only Hurts When I Serve*, Marlene Fanta Shyer writes: "I used to think that tennis elbow was nothing more than a sore arm, but now I know the difference."

She adds, "Tennis elbow means you can't turn on your car's ignition key, spray your hair, lift your glass of gin-and-tonic or spank your kids. Worst of all, you can't play tennis."

The United States Tennis Association, the national governing body for tennis in the US, reports that tennis injuries have been reported throughout all regions of the body with the shoulder, elbow, and knee being the most common areas of complaint. Most tennis strokes are hit in a repetitive pattern, which can lead to overuse injuries, and the USTA notes that most of the injuries in tennis can be defined as overuse injuries.

The USTA's recent review of the incidence of injury in tennis has found that injury rates are relatively low. For every one thousand hours an athlete is on the court practicing or competing, he or she is likely to incur two to twenty injuries. Compared with other sports, this is a very low injury rate, but injuries still exist in tennis, and many of these injuries are a result of poor preparation and training.

Joint injuries are the most common tennis injuries, the USTA says. The key to preventing injuries to the joints is to make sure the surrounding muscle groups and associated ligaments and tendons are strong and flexible. Acute injuries such as ankle sprains or bruises caused by collisions with fences or net posts can always occur, but proper training can help prevent many chronic injuries.

The most common types of overuse injuries in tennis occur to the shoulder from hitting thousands of serves and ground-strokes over time; the elbow, often related to improper technique or equipment; the lower back and abdominals, from twisting and turning over an extended period of time and hitting with a open stance; and the knees and hips because of the stopping and starting nature of the sport. In addition, the lower legs and feet can take a beating from regular play on hard courts and the frequent changes of direction during a match. The most common injuries of the lower legs and feet include calf strains, shin splints, and plantar fasciitis. As you can see, tennis injuries can happen to all parts of the body. The key is to strengthen the muscles surrounding each joint to help prevent many injuries.

A percentage comparison based on reported studies in tennis players shows that the lower extremity is the most frequently injured region in tennis players, followed by the upper extremity and the head/trunk.

The most frequently injured parts of the lower body were the lower leg, ankle, and thigh (upper leg), with the ankle sprain and thigh muscle strain (hamstring, quadriceps, and adductors) as the most frequent injuries. Upper extremity injuries were most frequently located in the elbow and shoulder regions, with tendon injuries of the shoulder and tennis elbow as the most frequent injuries in that region.

The USTA, fitness experts, and leading coaches believe a tennis-specific strength and conditioning program can play a key role in preventing common injuries in tennis players.

Rick Macci, who coached five players in their developmental years who became the top-ranked players in the world (Jennifer Capriati, Andy Roddick, Venus and Serena Williams, Maria Sharapova), points out that the game has changed dramatically in the past decade or so.

"I think because the game of tennis is so much faster and quicker and balls are coming at a higher velocity," Macci says, "there's a lot more torque on the body and people are hitting with a lot more angular momentum, where they're rotating their body so much faster. As a result there's a little bit more stress on the shoulder, on the elbow, and the arm. Those are probably the biggest injuries in general and they have gone to a whole new level.

"Now that being said, because the speed of the game is so much faster, and movement is such a premium, stopping and starting is taking more of a toll on your joints. So the change of direction has really affected the ankles, the knees, and the hips. This has become very common for a lot of stress on the back also.

"For any parent you want to first make sure you understand your medical history to prevent anything in the past genetically that maybe you've experienced, such as injuries when they were growing up, your relatives. You might be a little more prone for that to happen. The apple doesn't fall far from the tree. You see that's very common where someone will say I had shoulder problems when I was a kid too. Or I had this when I was that age also. I think just being proactive going into this is very critical."

Chuck Gately, a teaching pro of players of all levels and ages in New England and Florida for forty-five years, believes that 90 percent of tennis injuries are caused by the slice backhand and leading with the elbow.

Dr. Jonathan Hersch, an orthopaedic surgeon in South Florida specializing in sports medicine and arthroscopy, believes early detection of tennis elbow is key.

"Tennis elbow is a very common problem in recreational tennis players, but it in fact is an infrequent problem in accomplished tennis players," he says. "It's rare on the professional circuit to see a player with this condition. This injury occurs as a result of repetitive overload.

"The extensor tendon attachments to the elbow become injured over time. The symptoms include point tenderness over the lateral aspect of the elbow, pain with resisted wrist extension, pain upon gripping objects (lifting a gallon of milk is a common complaint) and pain on the backhand stroke.

"Mechanical and technical factors play a major role in the development of this problem. Unskilled players may have alterations in stroke technique that can place excess stress on the elbow. Leading with the elbow during the backhand and trying to place underspin on the ball with excessive pronation of the forearm are examples of techniques that can lead to this problem."

Dr. Hersch says many amateur players lack shoulder strength needed for continued play, especially the external rotators (part of the rotator cuff). This lack of strength causes the elbow extensor muscles to work harder, which leads to fatigue and tendon injury.

"Treatment focuses on reducing symptoms and improving mechanics," Hersch says. "Therapy starts with reducing the stress on the elbow and reducing inflammation which is present in the early phase.

"That may mean complete stoppage of play for several weeks, or in mild cases cutting back on the days and hours played until resolution of the pain. Early use of a counterforce tennis elbow strap can be helpful to reduce the stress on the involved tendons. This brace can also be used when returning to play on a preventative device. To reduce inflammation and pain, a cortisone injection may be recommended but requires rest from tennis for at least ten days to be effective. Multiple injections are discouraged due to the damage it can cause to tendons, worsening the problem.

"In most athletes, rest, ice, and anti-inflammatory medicines can cure this problem. Rehabilitation focuses on strength deficits in the shoulder, elbow, and forearm. Working with a certified physical therapist is recommended to ensure proper technique. Working with a tennis teaching professional can be a major help to improve mechanics and prevent further injury or recurrence.

"Failure to respond to treatment occurs in about 10 percent of athletes. For some, surgery is eventually recommended when all else fails. The surgical procedure can be done open or arthroscopically to remove the degenerative tissue involved. Arthroscopic surgery has the benefit of also allowing visualization of the inside of the elbow joint. Many people have other associated problems within the joint that can be treated simultaneously. On average, a return to tennis takes place about three months after surgery.

"If you believe you are suffering from tennis elbow, you should discuss this with a sports medicine professional. Early detection and treatment can result in resolution of the problem and minimal time away from the game you love."

In regard to wrist injuries, the problem is growing at the professional and advanced level. The surgeon who operated on pros Juan Martin Del Potro and Laura Robson insists that there are numerous reasons why wrist injuries are the prime concern among modern-day tennis players.

Dr. Richard Berger, an orthopedic surgeon at the Mayo Clinic in Rochester, Minnesota, has come to be regarded as the go-to man when wrist problems occur, according to *Bob Larson's Daily Tennis News*. The number of those afflicted has been high. In addition to the recovering Del Potro and Robson, several other pros, including Novak Djokovic and Caroline Wozniacki, have missed out on tournaments, and Sloane Stephens also experienced problems for much of 2014. Berger points out the fact that players are hitting the ball harder and harder, thanks to racquet technology, which puts far greater torque on the wrist and consequently the joint and its tendons are under increasing strain. "I do sense that more of the top players, the very elite touring pros, are probably experiencing injuries sufficient to take them out of the sport for some period in time at a higher rate," Berger says. "Tennis is one of those sports that, honestly, the wrist is one of the structures at most risk because the force of contact with the ball is transmitted directly through the wrist, and very often, with an element of torque as the player attempts to place higher and higher degrees of spin on the ball."

The fact that a large portion of current-day players operate predominantly from the baseline and employ a double-handed technique on the backhand heightens the risk of wrist problems, Berger reports. "You've got this overwhelming strength and speed in the players, that competitive drive that once they're out there playing, they're going to be playing as hard as they can against their opponents, and they can get into this vicious cycle of 'Well, I can outhit you.' But these structures are just so vulnerable."

To help you avoid injuries, select the proper racquet for your game, consider the type of surface you prefer to play on, and be wise in selecting shoes and clothing.

The USTA recommends consulting with a certified tennis instructor when finding a racquet appropriate for your game type, size, and strength. They note that taking a few lessons will help you learn proper stroke technique, which cuts down on the number of injuries.

They also recommend considering the type of surface on which you prefer to play. Clay and grass courts typically tend to be a bit more forgiving on the body than hard court surfaces, but clay court surfaces can require greater strength and flexibility in the hips and legs because of the sliding required to get to shots.

Shoe manufacturers make surface-specific shoes that are available at most sporting goods stores and tennis clubs. The USTA points out that the key to selecting a good tennis shoe is to make sure the shoe provides sufficient lateral support in addition to cushioning. A knowledgeable person at a sporting goods store or a certified tennis teaching professional should be able to advise you regarding the appropriate shoe for your game, body type, and court surface.

Also, because tennis is often played in warm environments, make sure you wear light-colored, loose-fitting clothing, and a hat or visor to protect you from the sun. Use sunscreen and properly hydrate before, during, and after play to prevent many problems and heat-related illnesses.

Yet fitness programs do more than just help tennis players avoid injuries. In fact, participating in such a program has many benefits, for players of all ages and skill sets. Here are five areas that can be improved with the integration of a program, according to Jeff Drock:

- Endurance: Tired players have the tendency to try to end points quickly with a winner or an error. Of course, this is usually a losing cause because it is nearly impossible for the tired player to get into proper positioning to execute effective strokes. When a player is physically fit, he or she has both the ability and confidence to be fresh throughout long matches. Therefore, fit players can hang in there and grind out point after grueling point.
- Pace: Stronger muscles allow players to hit the ball harder as well as handle harder-hit balls easier.
- Agility: The improved ability to be balanced and efficiently change directions will allow a player to chase down more balls during a match.
- Quickness/Balance: Getting to the ball is half the battle. The other half is moving and positioning the feet and body to set up for shots and hit them right in the strike zone.
- Increased confidence: With better movement, power, and endurance, a tennis player can become much more competent and confident in his/her playing ability.

FIRST STEP: THE DYNAMIC WARM-UP AND MOBILITY

I n their book *Complete Conditioning for Tennis*, the US Tennis Association's E. Paul Roetert and Todd Ellenbecker wrote that a high-quality conditioning program for tennis includes strength, flexibility, and anaerobic and aerobic training. "If tennis players neglect a component in their training program, they are unlikely to achieve their full performance potential and are more susceptible to injury while playing."

Research by the USTA and numerous strength and conditioning coaches has led to changes in the understanding of flexibility exercises and have identified the critical need for warm-up and dynamic stretching before playing tennis. Roetert and Ellenbecker point out that understanding the essential components of a proper warm-up and the differences between static stretching and dynamic stretching is important to achieving your best performance and at the same time minimizing the risk of injury.

They note that "the physical demands of playing tennis stress all regions of the body and as such, proper warm-up and flexibility training must include all areas of the body."

Among both recreational and elite players, injuries to the upper and lower extremities as well as the spine and torso have been reported. Therefore, the warm-up plays a key role in a tennis player's conditioning program. Warm-up exercises should be performed before flexibility work.

You warm up to prepare the body tissues to optimally respond to the exercises and stretches applied during the workout and to prevent injury.

As Roetert and Ellembecker point out, players should be encouraged to take part in a dynamic warm-up before playing tennis or high-intensity workouts and use static stretches after playing tennis. By incorporating stretches that target key areas of need and maintaining proper flexibility, players will prevent injury and enhance their performance.

How important is the warm-up for players of all ages and ability? Are players putting themselves at risk if they don't warm up? Those questions were posed to Bill Norris, who for more than forty years on the men's professional circuit treated everyone from Rod Laver to Jimmy Connors, as well as John McEnroe, Roger Federer, and Rafael Nadal.

"I believe that all ages and abilities benefit from a warm-up if you are practicing, playing a match, or taking a lesson," Norris said. "Without a thorough warm-up, the player risks injury.

I don't believe warm-ups differ by age groups and ability levels. We all have stiffness in our muscle groups no matter how old we are or how talented we are. We never want to get out there and risk a muscle strain due to improper warm-up."

Norris, who wrote the book *Pain, Set and Match* and now runs a consultancy in Boca Raton, Florida, where he treats young and old, was asked if warm-up routines differ for men and women, or for boys and girls.

"My answer is 'no' to both questions," Norris said. "Both men and women and boys and girls need to warm up their muscles. Most people need to soak in a hot tub or take a hot shower before doing some light exercise such as stretching, riding a stationary bike, jogging, or doing some calisthenics."

Should warm-ups for practice or a lesson be different than warm-ups for a match?

"No. The warm-up for both should include the tips I suggested in the previous question. You can also add stretches for the legs, back, upper body, wrists, arms, shoulder muscles, and neck muscles."

Can you recall examples of injuries when players didn't have a warm-up? Did some end up in a hospital?

"I have seen several examples of muscle injury due to improper warm-up before practices and matches. I have seen players having to go to the hospital for a ruptured Achilles tendon. This was a result of no warm-up to the lower leg."

Jeff Drock emphasizes that all players need to warm up their muscles.

"Begin with a very slow walking place, then slow jogging to medium jogging, and kind of a slow run," Drock said. "Someone else may forget walking and go from a medium jog to a slow run to a faster running pace and then sprint.

"Instead of static stretching, go with dynamic warm-up routines. Specific movements like high knees, butt kicks, lunges, shuffles, crossover steps, and all types of ladder drills are great for getting the system warmed up.

"Increasing the body temperature helps muscles become more pliable. Warming up also decreases the muscle viscosity, the fluid in the muscles. It's very thick in the muscles, the warm-up thins it out, the lubrication around the joints. And it reduces injuries. There's a lot of proof this enhances performance.

"The warm-up also prepares the heart and [allows the] blood vessels [to] adjust; it helps [the] cardiovascular system. Warming up even helps speed up the transmission of nerve impulses. If you warm up you're able to move much better. You also have a much better connection between the brain and the muscles.

"It increases blood flow to muscles, and that increases the delivery of nutrients for good energy production."

Drock believes warm-ups should not differ for men and women, or boys and girls, "except it's important to see what the ability and age of the athlete is. The much younger or older need to warm up in a slower manner. And the warm-up does not need to be for more than five to ten minutes. Whether you are warming up for a practice or lesson, I think the warm-up should be the same.

"With older players, especially those over thirty or thirty-five, if they don't warm up they will tend to get injured very frequently. That I see a lot. And the warm-up will help them perform better.

"For junior players it will help prevent injury, but what I see most is that it increases their performance."

Veteran tennis teaching pro Chuck Gately has worked for forty-five years with players of all ages and levels of ability in New England and Florida, and he believes there are some differences in how players in various climates should approach the warm-up.

"In New Hampshire: You have to get the blood circulating in the legs and the arms," he said. "It's much more important because if you don't, all of a sudden you're going to take that step and pull a muscle. I was born in New England and I was much, much more conscious of doing this, and it makes sense. Down here in Florida you're sweating like a pig, but up there you're protecting your heart and your lungs, your liver and kidneys."

Gately believes the warm-up plays an important part in a tennis player's conditioning program, saying, "Warm-up exercises should be performed before flexibility work. Recommended activities for warm-ups are, for example, jumping jacks, calisthenics, slow jogging in place, or arm circles. The recommended time frame for the warm-up is three to five minutes. Additional benefits are improved tissue elasticity and a reduced risk of muscle and tendon injury.

"Incorporating stretches that target key muscle areas such as hamstring, calf, quadriceps, groin, and lower back are essential. Senior tennis players should limit the intensity of their warm-up. And routines need not differ between men and women.

"Most club players engage in dynamic warm-ups before tennis play. However, they neglect the importance of static stretches after tennis play. In other words, so many people leave the court and they're tired and fatigued and they don't re-stretch out. They're good at doing basic stuff before they start, but they neglect doing it after.

"Players who play in cold climate regions are much more diligent with their warm-ups because the blood flows in their body to warm their organs, leaving the legs and arms with low blood supply. So they need the exercises for arms and legs to generate some blood supply to prevent injury.

"With an elite junior, it's so important to warm up. And the difference between a girl and a boy I don't think that should vary. We're not lifting weights here."

Gately added, "The most important thing here is [this—] the warm-up is entirely different than the stretching. Some people get confused. The warm-up should consist of running or jogging or something like that to get the blood flowing before they stretch."

Among the players he works with, Gately says that calf injuries are very prevalent. "Pulling a calf can be painful and that takes a long time to heal."

Hamstring injuries, Gately says, are probably the second most prevalent, and then quad injuries. Pulling a calf can be painful and that takes a long time to heal.

He also emphasizes the importance of starting slow and picking up speed when it comes to warming up the serve. "I always tell people in regard to starting to serve, I use the analogy of a pitcher in the bullpen. He warms up for several minutes before he throws hard. So you start off with a serve at half speed, then three-quarter speed and you gradually pick up. So many people hit that serve in the warm-up as hard as they're going to play in the match. You watch the pros, they take their time and gradually increase the pace of the ball."

Gately believes the warm-up for a match should be approached differently than practice, particularly for a good player. "The intensity, the amount of effort they're putting into the stroke is so much more. For those guys it's really important to do this. The club player isn't going to put nearly as much emphasis on the power. They're not going to swing as hard, there's less chance they're going to pull a muscle. For a club hacker it's important but not nearly as important than [for] the guy who's going to try to hit a forehand eighty miles an hour."

Dynamic Warm-Ups

A player may do all of the warm-ups depicted in this section and even add a few others of their own or their fitness coach's preference. When doing these or any exercises, it is necessary to get a doctor's medical clearance and perform these under the supervision of a fitness conditioning professional.

Start off with a three-minute jog around the court. This is to be done very slowly just to get the blood circulating through your system and your temperature increased.

The following dynamic warm-up exercises can easily be performed in less than ten minutes.

Carioca steps

The first is called **Carioca steps**, which help increase the circulatory function of the lower legs and trunk.

Cross the right foot over the left leg and then the right foot behind the left leg in an alternating fashion at a jogging speed.

Continue with the left leg going in front of the right and then behind in an alternating fashion at a jogging speed.

high knees

The **high knees** warm-up can help you improve circulation in the hips and trunk. Bring one knee up along with the opposite arm as if in a running motion; alternate legs. This is to be done at a jogging speed and can be done either stationary or while actually jogging.

over the hurdle

This one, known as **over the hurdle**, can help improve circulation in the hips and groin areas. Stand on either leg while bringing the other leg up. While the leg is up in the air, swing it horizontally. The knee should be kept even with the hip or higher if flexibility allows. Perform this movement between five and ten slow and controlled swings, and then perform this with the other leg.

walking lunge with side twist

If you're trying to improve circulation of the quadriceps and hips, the **walking lunge with side twist** is the exercise for you. While interlocking the hands or crossing your arms in front of your chest, lunge forward and twist slowly and comfortably to one side, then lunge to the other leg and twist in the other direction.

side lunge

The **side lunge** increases your circulation in the hip and groin areas. With feet wider than shoulder width apart, take a large step sideways and bend the leg you step with until you feel a gentle stretch in the groin area. The other leg should be straight. Repeat this movement between five and ten times and proceed with the opposite leg. The picture shows the end position of the side lunge (go as low as you comfortably can).

arm side swings

With these **arm side swings,** you can improve the circulation of your trunk, hips, and shoulders. Bring the arms out to the side and to shoulder height. Gently rotate the arms by twisting the trunk. Perform between 10 and 20 alternating twists. Note: Each player's flexibility will differ. Make certain these are performed in a slow and smooth manner.

wrist circles

Performing **wrist circles** improves circulation to the wrists and forearms. With one hand grab onto the fingers of the other and slowly and gently perform 5 circles in one direction and 5 circles in the other direction. Then perform this movement on the alternating hand. Perform 5 wrist circles in one direction and 5 circles in the other direction.

arm circles

This next warm-up, the **arm circles**, increases circulation in the shoulders. Bring arms straight out to the sides and even with your shoulders.

Slowly perform 5 circles forward and 5 circles backward. Begin with a very small range of circles and gradually make the circles bigger. Then perform 5 medium circles forward and 5 medium circles backward. Then perform 5 big circles forward and 5 big circles backward.

ankle circles

The **ankle circles** warm-up helps increase circulation of the ankles. Cross one leg over the other, grab onto the top of your shoe, perform 5 to 10 gentle ankle circles in one direction, and repeat in the other direction. Perform this exercise with the other ankle.

forward leg swings

Forward leg swings help increase circulation of the hip flexors. While keeping one foot on the ground, raise the other, slightly bending the knee. Kick the leg forward in front of the other foot and gently swing it back and forth 5 to 10 times. Perform this movement on the opposite leg. This should be done in a very comfortable fashion just to get the blood flowing in the hips.

side leg swings

This last one—**side leg swings**—increases circulation of the groin and hip areas. While keeping one leg straight and slightly bending the knee of the performing leg, gently swing the leg away from the hip and over your other foot 5 to 10 times. Perform this movement with the opposite leg.

Cardio Tennis

There is a form of tennis aerobics called Cardio Tennis which emphasizes getting one's heart rate into specific fat-burning and heart-healthy heart rate training zones. In this type of training, the activity can be extremely intense and a heart rate monitor is a necessary part of the program. Before taking part in this activity, specific warm-ups take place.

Cardio Tennis, a global brand recognized in more than thirty countries, is a rapidly growing program that emphasizes warm-ups and exercising. According to Michele Krause, Tennis Industry Association (TIA) Cardio Tennis Manager, Cardio Tennis is a high-energy fitness program that combines the best features of the sport of tennis with cardiovascular exercise, delivering the ultimate, full body, calorie-burning aerobic and anaerobic workout. The purpose is to train all zones of your body and burn calories. The Cardio Tennis experience includes training with a heart rate monitor, music, cardio balls, and the agility ladder, resulting in total mind and body engagement.

Among the benefits:

- Participants are able to achieve their effective heart rate zones with ease because of the "fun factor."
- You can burn more calories than you can by playing a singles or doubles match.
- It is a fun group activity where players of all ability levels enjoy tennis together.
- The primary focus is on getting a great workout. It helps fight the obesity crisis and offers a better fitness option for those not motivated to go to a workout gym.

Krause notes that all Cardio Tennis sessions start with a proper and progressive warm-up. A proper warm-up prepares the mind and the body for the demands of the activity as well as develops biomotor abilities within a given sport. The proper warm-up will also play in a role in injury prevention. Tennis players are notoriously very poor at warming up; it is the job of tennis professionals to educate them on what a proper warm-up looks like and its benefits. The warm-up in Cardio Tennis takes approximately ten minutes and should be intense where heart rates can reach 70 to 80 percent of maximum heart rate. There are three parts to a Cardio Tennis warm-up:

1) Active-Dynamic movement and stretching
2) Tossing and catching skills
3) Light hitting

- Active-Dynamic movement and stretching: Activities that will increase core body temperature while improving cardiovascular endurance through the integration of movement skills. Dynamic movement for tennis will include linear and lateral movement, crossover patterns, and multiple direction change. Examples include jogging, skipping, grapevine exercises, and hopping while incorporating large arm movements for maximum range of motion.
- Tossing and catching skills: Tennis is a sending and receiving sport (mostly receiving); therefore it is important that we train and develop our catching and tossing skills. These types of skills can be worked on dynamically in the warm-up and can also be addressed in a more static environment in the cool-down. These activities are delivered in engaging and challenging ways, in many cases taking the player outside their comfort zone. That is where the improvement occurs.
- Light hitting: Before we bang balls from the baseline, it is important to develop touch and feel for the ball with light hitting. Light hitting activities are typically done with shorter court boundaries using the red or orange Cardio Ball. These activities are often done with a partner and are very cooperative.

Krause emphasizes that by following this warm-up progression, you will be physiologically and psychologically prepared to play tennis.

EXERCISING TO PREVENT INJURIES

C hris Jordan, the Director of Exercise Physiology at the Johnson & Johnson Human Performance Institute in Orlando, Florida, says it is not unusual for individuals who work out in the gym religiously and consider themselves fit to subsequently walk out onto a tennis court in the sunshine and feel exhausted after just a few games! Why would someone who can run for hours on a treadmill and bench press more than their bodyweight struggle to play tennis for thirty minutes?

Your body adapts to the specific environment and the demands placed upon it. Lifting weights in an air-conditioned gym is very different from playing tennis in a hot, humid environment.

So how should you train?

Jordan says the goal is to improve your tennis-specific fitness. Your fitness is largely determined by three energy systems—stored, anaerobic, and aerobic. Each system can be associated with a type of activity: explosive (stored), intense for approximately 10–90 seconds (anaerobic), and continuous for 3-plus minutes (aerobic). You can increase the capacity of each system with appropriate training.

Your stored energy system is the most important when it comes to tennis, since most points in a tennis match last for just a few seconds. To improve the stored energy system you must overload it. To do this, perform repeated intense bursts of exercise up to 30 seconds followed by short rest periods. Use a 1:3 work/rest interval ratio.

Jordan offers a sample 30-minute treadmill workout: Warm up for 5 minutes, perform five 5-second sprints with 15-second rest intervals, five 10-second sprints with 30-second rest intervals, five 20-second sprints with 60-second rest intervals, and five

30-second sprints with 90-second rest intervals. Then cool down for 5 minutes.

To make your fitness training more tennis-specific, perform short work/rest intervals on the tennis court by running back and forth and side to side. Aim to closely mimic the movements you perform during a match. For example, sprint from the baseline or service line to the center of the net and back to the baseline and then repeat to the left and right sides of the net. Sprint back and forth the width of the court at the baseline and service line. Also, from the center mark, sprint back and forth to the center line, then diagonally toward the net.

Remember to wear loose, comfortable, and breathable clothing; hydrate regularly; and expose yourself gradually to the heat and humidity. Eat a sports bar one hour prior to playing, and consume eight ounces of a sports drink during the match every 15 minutes to replenish carbohydrates and rehydrate adequately.

US Tennis Association fitness and conditioning experts note that one of the unique things about tennis is that it stresses nearly all areas of the body. Although most people immediately think of tennis elbow as the ultimate tennis injury, the elbow is only one area commonly injured in tennis players. Injuries can arise in all parts of the body because of the nature and stresses of tennis; however, areas most frequently injured in elite players include the shoulder, lower back, hip, and knee. Data from the US Open Tennis Championships consistently identify the shoulder and back as the leading areas of injury.

How do you prevent a tennis injury from occurring? The answer is complex. USTA experts say the best way to prevent an injury is to condition yourself optimally for tennis and prepare your body for the stresses incurred in the game. Many health professionals and tennis coaches used to say, "Play tennis to get in shape." Although tennis certainly provides inherent fitness benefits to the heart, lungs, muscles, and bones, that philosophy doesn't reflect current thinking. USTA experts say the best way to prevent an injury is to condition yourself optimally for tennis and prepare your body for the stresses incurred in the game. The key to preventing injuries and optimizing performance in tennis, therefore, is clearly, "Get in shape to play tennis."

In addition to performing strength and flexibility exercises, using proper technique and selecting equipment appropriate for your playing style and body type also play a critical role. The racquet's stiffness, weight, grip size, and string tension are important to consider for injury prevention. Racquet stiffness refers to the amount of racquet deflection during ball impact. Frame material affects deflection, and therefore racquet stiffness. In general, moderately stiff racquets are recommended.

In addition to stiffness, the weight of your racquet is important. Use a racquet that has enough weight to absorb the stress of impact but not enough to make it difficult to maneuver.

The racquet's grip size has significant ramifications for injury prevention, as well.

String tension also plays an important part in injury prevention and in optimizing the performance of the racquet. Each racquet comes with a recommended range of string tensions that the manufacturer feels will cover most of the players who play with that particular frame. Although individual preferences exist, the general rule is that for any given string and racquet type, a tighter string tension will produce a more controlled response from the racquet, and a looser string tension produces more power from the racquet. This is contrary to what many players think. Playing with a racquet with a very high string tension may create greater stress on the wrist, elbow, and shoulder and lead to injury.

In addition to string tension, the material and type of strings affect performance as well. For injury prevention, strings that are made of many fibers, or filaments, provide greater resiliency and a generally superior feel.

LEGS: "MONEY-MAKERS IN TENNIS"

At the age of thirty-two, Andre Agassi worked as hard as ever to win Grand Slam tournaments against all of the top players in the world. Most of them were between five and ten years younger. And yet Agassi continued to crush all of his opponents. In the best-of-five-sets format, players must be physically prepared to play many five-set matches. How is it possible for a guy at the age of thirty-two to run down more balls and be in better court condition than they were at age twenty? As Agassi stated about his strength and conditioning coach Gil Reyes, "Without Gil I wouldn't be one-half of the player I am today."

Agassi became a huge role model for players looking to get the edge over their opponents. He added between fifteen and twenty pounds of muscle at the age of thirty-two than he had at the age of twenty. That added muscle equated to him being able to handle his opponent's pace better and hit the ball with more power. The added muscle and enhanced court coverage equated to quite a devastating package for his opponents. They sometimes felt like they were on the court against a freight train. Reyes and Agassi proved to be quite the team.

Keep in mind the fact that there are essentially four types of strokes that an opponent can hit to your side of the court:

1. Easy balls: balls hit to you, and you can attack these.
2. Neutralizing balls on which you can hit a decent shot back, but it is not time to go for a winner.
3. Defensive balls that you can barely get to and may have to stretch and reach for these, perhaps even throwing up a lob or slice in getting it back.
4. Winners, or shots that you are not going to be able to get to.

Thus, it becomes clear why Agassi's enhanced ability to get to the ball was so key. Getting to even a few more balls will greatly enhance a player's game. Agassi got to so many balls and was primarily in the offensive position. The opponents no longer played within themselves and oftentimes tried to hit winners from balls that they should have been neutralizing. This led to more errors, greater frustration levels, and a sure loss for the opponent.

Pat Etcheberry, a trainer for many of the top professional players on the tour and the former coach for Pete Sampras, Jim Courier, Sergi Bruguera, and others, put strength and conditioning for tennis on the map. He once made this very true comment: "Tennis is a running sport and the players' legs are their money-makers."

There are numerous exercises a player may do to enhance base leg strength levels. Some include functional weight training, running sprints up hills, sprints in sand, sprints with a parachute, sprints with an elastic cord, and weighted sled pulling.

Enhancing anaerobic endurance is what strengthens the heart muscle and creates the endurance necessary to keep fresh for long matches and tournaments. This can be achieved by participating in repeated sprints with minimal rest times. Doing repeated 800-, 600-, 400-, 200-, and 50-meter sprints can achieve this.

A warning: Incorporate sprints into your routine at a pace that suits you (usually a slower one for beginners). Do not go to the track and immediately try to do the 20x200-meter workout because you may not be able to get up off the track when you are done. Doing various on-court agility and quickness drills with cones, medicine balls, and agility ladders will also be quite helpful.

A Healthy Shoulder Promotes Good Tennis

Why when I serve or hit overheads do I get shoulder pain? is a question that most tennis players contemplate at some point in their career.

Dr. Jonathan Hersch provides an answer:

"There are several sources of shoulder pain in tennis players," he says. "During tennis strokes, especially the serve, there are repeated stresses on the shoulder that occur. One of the most common causes is bursitis or tendonitis. The rotator cuff muscles are a group of four muscles and tendons that control the rotation of the shoulder during motion. In addition they help maintain the stability of the ball and socket joint of the shoulder.

"The tendons are surrounded by a bursa or protective sac of fluid that over time can develop inflammation from impingement against the surrounding bone. This can cause pain especially when reaching overhead during a serve. As the muscles get tired, they don't function properly and this inflammation can get worse, causing a cycle of pain if not treated.

"First, it is important to know how to prevent these problems. Increasing strength and endurance of the shoulder muscles is an important part of prevention of shoulder injury. Under the guidance of a therapist or trainer, simple exercises can be learned to be performed several times a week to prevent the development of shoulder pain and impingement. Any increases in playing time should be done on a gradual basis so as not to overload the shoulder. It is overuse that causes the most problems."

For those who experience persistent shoulder pain, Hersch advises beginning treatment to get better and not playing through the pain. As Hersch explains, "The first aim of treatment is to reduce the inflammation in your shoulder rapidly and safely. Rest and ice application can usually do this in most cases of early impingement. Rest means stop playing. Most tennis players don't want to be told that, but it is necessary for at least a short period of time. Anti-inflammatory medications can be used but with caution and in short periods so as to avoid the common side effects on the stomach.

"Once the pain and inflammation have resolved, restoration of range of motion and strength should begin. This should be under the supervision of a physician and therapist/trainer to make sure the exercises are done properly. A gradual return to tennis would be allowed when full pain-free motion occurs."

Hersch explains that if this treatment does not work, then surgery may be necessary. Other causes of shoulder pain, such as instability (looseness of the shoulder) and labrum tears, may require a visit to a sports medicine specialist.

He concludes, "A healthy shoulder promotes successful tennis."

Guiding Junior, College Players

Veteran tennis coach Chuck Gately, who has worked with players of all levels for forty-five years, often has the following conversation when advising junior players about injury prevention:

"I tell the kids, 'How often do you take a bath? Once a day or once a month?'"

"'I take a bath once a day, coach.'"

"'Well that's the time. You take that bath and you get down on the floor and you do your pushups. Don't you ever come to me and say 'I don't have time.'"

In other words, complete your pushups every day before bathing.

Gately continues, "The other thing I tell all the parents: Get a chinning bar for pull-ups and chin-ups. That strengthens the forearms. You don't need to lift weights. By doing just their own body weight they're not going to hurt themselves. And do it at least three times a week. It helps prevent injuries in their shoulder and their elbow. And I try to tell the parents, don't make it too laborious so they don't want to do it.

They're not going to come out and do fifty pushups. If you can do five, do them."

Fitness and conditioning guru Pat Etcheberry once received a question from Lin Loring, head women's tennis coach at Indiana University and the most winning coach in Division I women's tennis, about preventing injuries through proper strength and conditioning training. During his thirty-three-plus years of coaching, he found that it is very common for freshmen and sophomores to get injured in college and be out for awhile. He noted that is the same age (18–19) that all the girls that turn pro are off the tour. Apparently, at that age, all the pounding seems to catch up with them and they fall apart. He asked Etcheberry for his thoughts.

His response: "The earlier junior players learn to train the muscles needed specifically for tennis, the better chance they have of avoiding injury when they enter their mid to late teens. This has to begin by high school. Many players see injuries spring up when they are sixteen to twenty years old because they haven't done the proper injury prevention training when they were younger. An injury to a young player often becomes a chronic problem throughout the player's career, or ends it. The way to avoid this is to initiate the proper training at younger ages.

"Preventing injuries early on is facilitated by coordinating the training to meet each of your players' specific needs and characteristics. Is the player strong? Is she quick? Is he tall or short? And what [exercises] do they need [that are] tennis-specific for their game? Start age-appropriate training early on to meet the specific needs of that individual player, and that will assure that they have the proper muscles needed for the game of tennis their entire lives."

Etcheberry believes both boys and girls share a need to strengthen their shoulders, back, and abdominal area early on in their development to prevent injuries and allow them to perform at their optimal level for years to come. I prefer using medicine ball drills and bench exercises with junior players to work the core of the body. They're healthful for everyone and help prevent back injuries. Plus, they have the tennis-specific advantage of resulting in a more functional strength that allows players to swing their racquet better.

As coaches, we need to remember that sometimes we train girls differently than we do boys, and that requires using exercises that recognize the gender distinctions in their muscle groups. For example, girls tend to develop more knee problems because they have smaller quads than boys, and that can result in more frequent knee injuries. The lunges and medicine ball exercises I use help develop the young players' quads and reduce the risk of knee injuries. Boys, on the other hand, seem to be more prone to injury in the wrist area because they often play with western grips, which place added pressures on the wrist that commonly lead to ligament and tendon problems later on. The wrist curl exercises help combat this. And they have the advantage that they can be started at an early age with lighter weights, increasing the weight as the player matures.

Another important aspect of injury prevention is simply communications. Specifically, communications between the four key elements in a young player's career: the player, the tennis coach, the fitness coach, and the player's parents. They are each part of the "team," and they need to communicate among themselves so that the player is not being over-trained. All parties need to converse so that the player is not doing so much on-court and so much off-court that we are burning her out or wearing him down. That's when injuries occur, or careers are destroyed.

Remember, the purpose of training in the first place is to produce a stronger, quicker tennis player who is free of injury when they enter the important years, from fifteen to adulthood. Coaches, but equally importantly parents, need to understand that pushing a child to win when they are ten or twelve does little for the player if they become injured by age sixteen and are forced to give up the game they love.

What to Eat, Drink, and Wear

Long-time ATP Tour trainer Bill Norris, in his book *Pain, Set and Match* (written with Richard Evans), notes that the more time you spend on a tennis court, or indulge in any energetic physical activity, the more various parts of your body are going to start crying "Help!" Muscles, ligaments, joints, and even bones are going to start complaining.

Sooner or later—and sooner if you play on hard courts—everyone who plays tennis consistently is going to develop some kind of physical problem. The problem can be minimized with proper treatment but the best way to handle the whole issue is through preparation and prevention.

Preparation does not start on the day of your match, but rather the night before. Some will say that days before that big match you need to prepare. Be careful of what you eat and be sure you drink plenty of fluids. The body needs time to absorb what you put into it and chugging a pint of water half an hour before you go on court is not going to do it.

So pick from the following:

Drinks: Drink water, fruit juice, vegetable juice, and sports drinks that contain trace minerals (sodium, potassium, calcium, magnesium, etc.).

Fruits: Eat fruits such as all melon, cantaloupe, pineapple, peaches, and blueberries in small amounts.

Vegetables: Consume veggies that are water-based, such as lettuce, carrots, celery, potatoes, jicama, radishes, spinach, and tomatoes.

Carbohydrates: Pasta, rice, and couscous are good for you.

Main meal: Fish, chicken, turkey, or lean beef are good the night before.

Breakfast: The morning of the match you may want to eat fruit, some carbs like cereal with very little milk, oatmeal, two pancakes, or cream of wheat or cream of rice.

Norris says a player needs to allow sufficient time to digest the food for it to be converted into fuel. The food that you eat tonight will be converted into fuel for tomorrow's match. If you are eating breakfast at 7 a.m., this will be fueling your afternoon's match.

Before the match, when you wake up, get into a hot bath or take a shower. The shower raises your core temperature. You want to be warm when you do your stretching. Norris points out that muscles react the same way as plastic. Cold plastic breaks, but heated plastic is malleable and will not break, just like a muscle.

Rub some analgesic balm into your shoulder, forearm, legs, and lower back, Norris says. For foot care and preventing blisters, take a tube or jar of Vaseline and apply some topically with a thin coating to the balls of your feet, heels, toes, and other areas where you will get friction. You can sprinkle some baby powder on top of the Vaseline. He suggests you put your socks on very carefully over your toes, making sure there are no wrinkles in the sock. If you have wrinkles, you might get a blister, so smooth out the wrinkles. For athletes that are prone to bruising of their feet, you may want to try a thicker sock. Plan to bring an extra pair of socks and an extra pair of tennis shoes to change into for longer matches. You also need to bring two backup tennis shirts and shorts, and throw in a warm-up suit to wear after the match while you are cooling off.

During the match, continue to drink sports drinks and water on changeovers.

In hot conditions you need to wear a hat. Playing outside you will need to apply a sun block of not less than 50 SPF. Even in overcast weather, one can get an adverse reaction to the rays, which penetrate the clouds.

Sun can really harm you, so take the proper precautions. After your match and practice, it is a good idea to cool down with a cold shower or ice bath. This will help to reduce inflammation and to relax your body.

Head to Toe

In regard to preparation and prevention, Norris also offers further tips, from your feet to your neck:

- **SHOES:** Think of your shoes as top-of-the-line tires. They have to absorb the battering and movement you put them through. The tread and the pressure have to be right. When selecting shoes, first feel them; squeeze them to see how they flex because the way they flex has a direct bearing on whether they are the right shoe for your feet. There are different treads made to accommodate different playing surfaces. If you usually play on hard courts and you're going off to play on American green clay or European red clay, you will need a different type of shoe. The same is true for playing on grass. If you are serious about your game, don't let money become a factor if you can afford the extra dollar. Get the shoe that fits you, even it if it is more expensive.
- **FOOT:** Tennis players will inevitably suffer foot problems. Your feet take a pounding on any type of surface, but because there's more play on hard courts these days, it's a matter of feet first when it comes to treating routine problems. As with all injuries, use ice to control swelling and pain. If pain persists, contact your physician. To prevent athlete's foot, wash and dry your feet immediately after a match or practice, then apply foot powder or baby powder to the bottoms of your feet and between the toes and sprinkle some inside your shoes. Change into clean dry socks, and let your shoes dry after practice and matches. Never wear wet shoes.
- **ANKLE:** Norris has dealt with all kinds of injuries during his lengthy career, but nothing has been as constant as ankle injuries on both the men's and women's pro tennis tours. He tells his players who roll an ankle to not take the tennis shoe off. Instead, tighten the laces. If the player takes the shoe off, the ankle will swell immediately. Leave it on to have compression on the foot and ankle until an athletic trainer can attend to you. If you are alone or where there

is no athletic trainer on site, you are better off submerging the entire shoe, encasing the foot, in a bucket filled with ice and water for twenty minutes. Take it out for twenty minutes and elevate the ankle to a height where it is higher than your hips and your heart. Then have the ankle medically checked unless it is a very mild sprain. If your ankle is treated correctly you can avoid down time and be able to return to competition in a few weeks. If you don't take care of this injury properly, you could be out of action for several months. RICE is the proper treatment for an acutely sprained ankle: rest, ice, compression, and elevation.

An ankle can break in tennis if it is turned severely with great force. This happens when a player goes for a shot and steps on a tennis ball or in doubles play steps on his/her partner's foot. If the player is going for a ball and suddenly changes direction, the player can suffer a fractured ankle. Common signs of a broken ankle include a recurrent diffuse ache in the ankle that increases with exercise, followed by pain-free periods, limited movement, and ankle bruising. See a sports medicine physician to get back on the tennis courts in a safe and timely manner.

- **LOWER LEG:** Players of all levels suffer injuries to the calf or lower leg at some time. Shin splints are pains on the inner side of the shin. Tennis players complain of this pain most when they play on hard courts or transition from playing on clay to hard courts. You need to seek medical advice from your physician for treatment. If the twisting and over-stressing of the shinbone is severe and is repeated enough times, the bone will crack. Many junior players develop stress fractures because their growth plates are open and bones are not fully developed. In the calf, tears commonly occur in the major muscles. This usually occurs when there has not been a proper or long enough warm-up. If you have an injury to the calf and lower leg muscles, use RICE. Calf cramps usually occur after stressful exercise and may be triggered by electrolyte imbalance, improper diet, lack of conditioning, illness, or dehydration.

- **TENNIS ELBOW:** Norris sees this many times when he treats club players. This condition results when the lateral muscles and tendons in the outside of the forearm have not been strengthened enough to handle the wear and tear of hitting tennis balls. Seek medical attention to get a proper diagnosis for treatment. Tennis elbow has an average duration of twelve to fifteen months.
- **HAND AND WRIST:** Sore wrists are very common in tennis and may be sprained or sore from overuse. Tendinitis can be treated if you get to it early. Icing after playing will help.
- **NECK:** Hitting an overhead or a serve can pull a neck muscle. To treat this you need to ice the stiff side and then gently stretch the neck away from the stiff side. The best way to prevent a neck injury is to strengthen your neck muscles.

EXERCISES TO PREVENT INJURIES

To help avoid the aforementioned aches and pains, here are some recommended exercises:

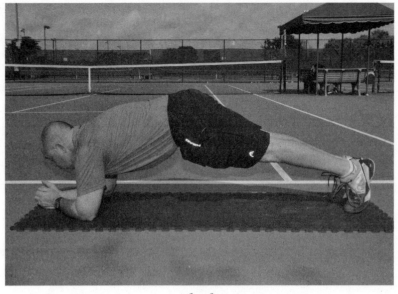

plank

The plank exercise focuses on improving core strength. The core is made up of all the muscles that connect the lower and upper body. Start on the elbows and knees while locking the hands together. Straighten the legs and raise your body so you are supported by the balls of your feet. Make certain to keep the feet hip distance apart and face the floor while being certain not to arch your back or stick your glutes in the air. Hold this position between 30 seconds and 1 minute as prescribed by your strength and conditioning coach. In order to perform a more advanced moving plank, simply bring your hips up a few inches and then come back to the starting position. Repeat for the desired amount of repetitions.

side plank

The **side plank** improves the core, with an emphasis on the oblique muscles. Lie on your right side propped up on your elbow, with the left foot resting on top of the right one. Push yourself up so that your body forms a triangle. Hold the position for the desired amount of time, and repeat on the other side. Note: You may perform these in a more advanced manner by slowly lowering yourself toward the ground and then back to the side plank position for the desired amount of repetitions as prescribed by your strength and conditioning specialist.

superman

The **superman/superwoman** exercise improves lower back strength and spinal erector strength. Lie facedown on the ground with arms out and straight overhead and your legs out straight behind you. Raise your chest and upper legs off of the ground. Try to get your chest and legs as high as possible. Make sure not to bend your knees. Keep your neck in a neutral position in exact alignment with the rest of your body. Pause while your arms and legs are off of the ground. Return your body to the starting position and continue for 12 to 20 repetitions.

medicine ball lunge with a torso twist

The **medicine ball lunge with a torso twist** enhances quadricep strength, hip flexor flexibility, and core strength. Stand with your feet shoulder width apart. Hold the medicine ball in front of you. Step forward with one leg into a lunge position and twist your upper body to the side from your torso toward the forward leg. Move your arms back to the center, step forward with the opposite leg, and twist to the other side. Continue this walking lunge/twisting movement for a desired amount of steps or distance (e.g., across the width or length of the court).

medicine ball chest pass on one leg

The **medicine ball chest pass on one leg** improves the core strength and stability of the chest, shoulder, quadriceps, hip flexors, and ankles. Grab a medicine ball and hold it with both hands in front of the chest. Palms should be facing each other with the thumbs pointing toward your face. Stand on one leg, which should be slightly bent, with the other leg slightly in front of the grounded leg. Throw the ball against the wall or to a partner (same motion as a chest pass in basketball). To make this exercise more challenging, perform it while standing on a BOSU®, a balance board, or in a sand pit (e.g., a beach or volleyball court).

bear crawl

The **bear crawl** improves the strength of the shoulders, quadriceps, core muscles, chest, and triceps. Proper technique begins with starting in the pushup position; then place the hands directly under the shoulders and rise up onto the balls of your feet. Move your right hand and left leg forward, then move your left hand and right leg forward. Try not to let the knees touch the ground. Continue for the desired amount of distance and/or times.

stability ball hamstring curl

The **stability ball hamstring curl** improves hamstring strength, glutes strength, and core strength and stability. Lie face up with the legs straight and heels on a stability ball. Contract the glutes to raise the hips; then pull your heels toward your body. Make sure not to let your hips drop as you pull your heels toward your body in order to move the ball toward you. Slowly extend your legs and repeat the exercise for the desired number of repetitions, generally between 12 and 15. This may also be performed with one leg at a time (the non-working leg would be slightly raised up off of the ball).

calf raises

Calf raises help enhance your strength and stability of your calves, ankles, and achilles tendons. Stand on the edge of a step or any slightly elevated and stable area. The balls of your feet should be firmly on the step or mat while your heels hang off of the edge. Raise your heels a few inches above the step until a calf contraction is felt. Lower the heels down to slightly below the level of the step/mat. When initially doing this exercise you may touch a wall or fence for balance, but the goal is to do these without holding onto anything. Some advanced progressions include performing these one leg at a time or while holding dumbbells. Perform 12 to 25 repetitions.

palms-down wrist curl

Similarly, the **palms-down wrist curl** strengthens the forearm extensors and the wrists. Sit on the end of a bench or stability ball and hold one dumbbell in your right hand. The wrist should be against your knee, with palm facing down. Raise the dumbbell up by raising only your hand, and slowly lower it back down. The arm should be kept still throughout the exercise. Repeat this on the other side. Perform this for 12 to 20 repetitions.

palms-up wrist curl

The **palms-up wrist curl** strengthens the forearm flexors and the wrists. Sit on the end of a bench or stability ball and hold one dumbbell in your right hand. The wrist should be against your knee, with palms facing up. Raise the dumbbell up by raising only your hand and slowly lower it back down. The arm should be kept still throughout the exercise. Repeat this on the other side. Perform this for 12 to 20 repetitions.

band external shoulder rotation

The **band external shoulder rotation** strengthens the external rotators of the shoulder. Stand with legs slightly wider than shoulder width apart and bend the knees slightly. Stand sideways to the point where the band is attached to the fence. Grab the band with the arm farthest away from the point of attachment. While keeping the elbow at 90 degrees, slowly bring your arm across the body and then back to the starting position shown in the picture. Perform 12 to 15 repetitions.

band rows

Band rows help to strengthen the mid and upper back. Grab a band and have your working arm straight out in front of you. Now pull the elbow along the torso and just slightly behind the back. This should be a straight line pull to a point just below your chest. Now extend the elbow to a nearly straight position, so your arm is completely straight, to complete one repetition. Make certain that you are standing in an athletic posture, with knees slightly bent and feet slightly wider than shoulder width apart. Perform 12 to 15 repetitions on each arm.

(Not pictured) **Elevated heel sand walking** strengthens stability of the calves, ankles, and achilles tendons. Simply walk around a sandy area while standing on the toes. Perform this for 30 to 90 seconds.

CHAPTER 4

PREVENTING INJURIES WHILE ON THE COURT

I n coaching countless players, from beginners to five who would become number 1 in the world, Rick Macci learned a basic and presumably simple fact that players overlook: Many tennis athletes seem to ignore the risk associated with tripping over a ball that shouldn't be on the court.

"One of the more common problems is people stepping on a tennis ball," he said. "I tell this to the kids all the time when they're in such a hurry. They hit the first serve, it hits the net, trickles back, and it's around the service box, wherever, and they just want to go ahead and play. And unfortunately until you step on a ball and turn your ankle, you may not learn. And I've had two people break their ankle completely. And believe me, you won't play with another ball on the court in life before you do anything.

"This is the number-one problem when kids play with a ball on the court and they turn an ankle. And a lot of times that can turn into a fracture. You never think you're going to step on it, but I've seen it happen hundreds and hundreds of times. Even going backwards by the fence, you're going to step on a ball. That would be the number-one precaution that you need to take, because when you step on a ball it can become very serious."

Satoshi Ochi, the USTA's Head Strength and Conditioning Coach in the Player Development program, concurred.

"Tennis balls on the court? Get them off," Ochi said. "Absolutely. You play with untied shoelaces, or you have tennis balls around [you create potential injury situations]."

Though Macci argues that the existence of the tennis balls on the court is a prevalent issue for kids, he states that for seasoned players, there are plenty of other risks. "For the more advanced player, I think there is a higher probability of an injury because of the frequency of the balls. You're going to get more repetitions, and the velocity of the ball is a lot faster, and you're going to be generating more torque on all the joints. So, I think there probably are a lot more of these injuries on the WTA Tour and the ATP Tour than in junior tennis just because it's more violent. It's like college and pro football, there are just more injuries in pro football because there are more intense, chaotic collisions that occur on a regular basis."

Macci added, "Believe me, professional athletes train differently. Their bodies are different, they're bigger, they're stronger, faster. But it cuts both ways. Even though pro tennis players are doing everything they can to stay in the best shape they can to prevent injuries, a lot of times it's just unavoidable pounding on hard courts, the wear and tear.

"On a clay court it's much easier. So, for older people they should focus on playing on a softer surface because it's easier on the knees and all the joints. And a lot of it is genetic. Look at Roger Federer. He's still playing and he has not had a lot injuries all through his career. He moves differently. He flows, he has more of a graceful game, where someone like Rafael Nadal is more violent, more of a grinder. And he's just pounding.

Ochi suggested that the court itself is not the only place where the injuries manifest. He said, "Also in the weight room when you are doing fitness, be aware. Unfortunately you see some accidents during fitness workouts, and sometimes you could easily avoid it. Do you have enough space? Are you using the right equipment? I think that applies to everybody."

Ultimately, though, Macci said that intangibles also factor into a tennis player's propensity for injury, which makes it even more important to be physically prepared. "A lot of it is your game style and a lot of it is genetics. And a lot of it could be luck of the draw. You go out there and just have bad luck. All these things go into it. You want to do everything possible to get the best advice, and prevention is probably the best remedy."

When to Stop a Match

Norris emphasizes the importance of knowing when to stop in a match, despite a player's feeling of invincibility or acknowledging their vulnerability. He maintains that in the long run, it's better for your body to have stopped when you first recognize the problem than to experience the long-term repercussions.

He points to several hard and fast signs that tell you to stop, including: dizziness, chest pressure, pain emanating down the arm, possible shortness of breath, feelings of weakness, perhaps even a sense of impending doom, or pain that hinders your running ability.

Norris also cites tingling or numbness in legs or pain radiating from the butt to the calf and foot if you have been diagnosed with sciatica as a sign to stop, in addition to or the absence of perspiration on a hot day, which could be a sign of hyperthermia, even during a shorter match.

He adds, "Exhaustion and trouble staying on your feet can be due to any number of things including hyperthermia, and muscle problems. Your body is telling you to stop playing and get medical care." Norris also cites the importance of bringing along an extra shirt and shorts. He recommends wearing a warm-up suit during the post-match cool-down.

Heat-Related Illness

USTA fitness and conditioning officials point out that heat stress is a common ailment during tennis play. It can include heat cramps, heat exhaustion, and, most seriously, heatstroke. The most widely recommended prevention strategies for heat illness are proper hydration and nutritional intake.

Contrary to popular belief, sport scientists now believe that sodium loss through heavy sweating may be the largest contributor to heat cramps.

Proper hydration involves drinking *before* you are thirsty and properly hydrating before tennis play. Drinking fluids the night before and early in the day before tennis play improves a player's pre-match hydration status.

Fitness and conditioning expert Jeff Drock recommends during actual playing time to take a few sips of your drink during every changeover, even if you are not thirsty. Players should never force themselves to drink large amounts of water or other beverages, he adds, because doing so can cause serious problems with your body's ability to regulate or balance electrolytes. This imbalance from drinking an over-abundance of water is called hyponatremia, and this can cause serious illness or even death. Contrary to popular belief, sport scientists now believe that sodium loss through heavy sweating may be the largest contributor to heat cramps.

Therefore, during periods of heavy sweat loss, replacement of sodium becomes important. Salt pills are not recommended and irritate the stomach and intestine. Before matches that will take place in high humidity conditions, make certain to salt foods more heavily and take electrolytes during the match.

Drock believes hydration is number one in terms of preventing problems on the court: "If you don't have access to a fountain, bring water. Hydrate during every changeover. The amount depends. At least a few sips to replenish. Even if you're not thirsty it's important to take a few sips. If you're thirsty it's a sign of dehydration. Maybe have water and a solution like Gatorade, or a hydration-type drink.

"Water's taste can get old. Gatorade and several sports drinks are very good with flavor and electrolytes. No beer or milk or dairy products. Alcohol impairs and leads to dehydration, not to mention tripping on a ball or over your own feet."

RESEARCHING THE NATURE OF INJURIES

In recent years we've seen a proliferation of injuries on the men's and women's professional circuits. One has to ask whether or not there are new ingredients in today's game that might be producing more injuries. Renowned coach, researcher, and author Vic Braden came to that conclusion when he and Dr. Gideon Ariel were recording physical forces in tennis in their research center in Southern California. They were surprised to discover that sudden turns by tennis players on a force plate could often produce 5 g's of force on the human body—that's five times the normal amount of gravitational pull. In today's game, new, light, and stiff racquet frames, along with improved strings, has greatly reduced the amount of time that elapses between hits. In some cases, the ball has to be hit by player A, and again by player A, in two seconds. That compares to the normal four to six seconds in the old days of wood racquets.

If such forces only occurred a few times in a match, it might not be so dangerous. However, today's players are constantly forced to make a sudden stop and quick turn-around to get a shot 27 feet away. The human body is only constructed to take so much punishment.

In the era of more open-stance players, we are seeing several pros hitting off the back foot. When Braden and Dr. Ariel studied former ATP Tour player Guga Kuerten hitting off the back foot, they tried to replicate the forces using a force plate. Braden said it was easy to see why players were getting ankle, knee, groin, and hip injuries.

"And it came as no surprise that Kuerten ended his career with a hip replacement," Braden said. "We had predicted serious injuries to Rafael Nadal and those predictions came true several times in his career. Nadal has often hit on the back foot on both the forehand and backhand."

In another study, the duo examined the forces projected on the wrist when there was a pre-stretch forehand style involved.

A pre-stretch forehand is characterized by the player's hitting arm moving forward while the wrist and racquet go back in the opposite direction during the initial stages of the forward arm movement.

This system pre-stretches the forearm muscles and generates tremendous racquet speed with a short backswing. A short backswing is now needed by the pros due to the rapid ball speed.

Braden and Dr. Ariel's study was generated due to a wrist injury on Andre Agassi, who used a pre-stretch system. As a result of their findings, it came as no surprise to them to see Juan Martin Del Potro exit tournaments complaining of a sore wrist.

"His fabulous forehand is characterized by a pre-stretch motion on the backswing and initial forward arm movement," Braden said. "If you watch some slow motion of a player's forehand, watch for the arm and racquet going to opposite directions at the furthest point on the backswing. The pre-stretch forehand is very common in today's tennis.

"It might be that exercise physiologists will have to restructure some training systems to accommodate the new features in stroke production of professional players. In the meantime, don't be surprised if the injury list continues to grow."

Braden believes the problem with so many players dropping out of tournaments is twofold: too many tournaments and balls traveling too fast. Sporting goods companies have spent millions of dollars developing racquets that could produce more speed with the same swing.

"What we now have is a racquet that can hit fast-traveling balls but greatly reduces forces on the arm and body at the same time," Braden said.

In a study by the Junior Tennis Ambassadors science team under the direction of Braden, the team determined that the time between hits for men was 2.2 seconds and for women 2.5 seconds. That means a male player who is hitting at the end of the doubles alley will have only 2.2 seconds to reach the opposite alley and get into proper position to strike the opponent's shot. That means amazing forces are placed on the leg used to stop and do a quick turn-around, not to mention the necessary foot speed to achieve that goal. The same extreme forces also apply to women, and the number of injuries to women has increased dramatically.

"I applaud the manufacturers' efforts to give the players what they demanded," Braden said. "What is missing in this scenario is that the new racquets have made millions of average players feel like Roger Federer. Mission accomplished, but what lies next?"

Braden had a couple of average players run the 36-foot width of the court in 2.2 seconds and then change directions each time. After only completing the exercise for three points, the players were practically begging him to stop.

THE COOL-DOWN AND FLEXIBILITY

T hough your tennis match may be over, your work is not. Or at least it shouldn't be, according to experts in the field. Your cool-down—the recovery time for stretching and working on flexibility—is vitally important.

Renowned fitness and conditioning expert Pat Etcheberry notes that tennis players and their coaches always plan for tournaments. They train and prepare both on the tennis court and in the gym based on their tournament schedules. However, many of the players that I talk with have no idea of how to plan for recovery between matches to allow them to stay fit yet physically reach the later rounds of the tournament without being sore, tired, or dehydrated.

What a player does after a match is critical to how they will play the next match. For starters, a good cool-down after the match will help you to start recovering quickly. Jim Courier was ahead of his time when, years ago, he would go for a jog after his matches. A lot of people thought he did this to impress other players, but in actuality he jogged to prevent soreness and to aid recovery both physically and mentally.

Nowadays all of the big tournaments have a gym on site for the players. This allows the player to get a good warm-up before the match as well as a cool-down after the match. If you check these gyms at the tournaments you will find that they have become quite popular.

Ideally, after a match you want to cool down with a light jog or a bike workout. The intensity should be low, and the exercise should only be performed for 10 to 15 minutes. This should be followed by a good total body stretching session. Afterwards, perform any rehab or treatment to prevent any past injuries from recurring.

As soon as possible after the match, the player should also start rehydrating with an electrolyte replacement fluid. In addition, the player needs to eat a healthy meal soon after the match's completion.

A massage is an excellent way to help the muscles recover faster and a nap, when possible, is a great help. A good night's sleep is also a must.

If you follow the above suggestions, your body will be better prepared to perform at a high level for the duration of the tournament.

Just a few minutes of recovery planning and follow through will allow you to be ready both physically and mentally for your next match.

Fitness trainer Jeff Drock notes that stretching during your cool-down "is great for working on your flexibility. During the cool-down you can do a very light jog. It's a great way to ease the body down, maybe for 10 minutes.

"After that, do stretches. Many players on the tour do 10-plus minutes. Go easy, do not push or make it difficult, and do this until you feel mild discomfort."

Cool-Down and Flexibility Exercises

Do these flexibility exercises under the close supervision of a coach or strength and conditioning specialist:

cross-arm stretch

The **cross-arm stretch** improves flexibility of the shoulders and upper back. Stand holding your right arm straight out in front of you; place your left arm behind your right left elbow. With the left arm pull the right arm across your body. Perform this exercise on the other arm.

overhead shoulder stretch

The **overhead shoulder stretch** improves flexibility of the shoulder and trapezius. Put the right arm straight up in the air; with the left arm grab the right elbow or just above it and gently push the arm backward. Repeat on the other arm.

wrist flexion

The **wrist flexion** exercise improves wrist flexibility. With your left hand grab the top of your right hand and gently press down on the hand. Repeat on the other side.

forearm extension

The **forearm extension** improves flexibility of the wrist and forearm. With your left hand, grab your right hand and gently press down on the hand. Repeat on the other side.

standing hamstring stretch

The **standing hamstring stretch** improves flexibility of the hamstrings. Stand with feet wider than shoulder-width apart, fold your body over until your hands touch the ground, and "walk" your hands over to your right foot, then left foot, and then the middle. (If you cannot touch the ground, then simply stretch until you feel a mild pull.) By placing the feet even wider than the picture shown, but performing the same exercise, you can effectively stretch the groin area.

Piriformis stretch

The **Piriformis stretch** improves flexibility of the piriformis muscle. Lie on your back with your left knee bent. Place the right ankle just above the left knee, and slowly pull the right leg toward the chest to feel the stretch in the right glute muscle. Repeat on the other side.

iliotibial band stretch

The **iliotibial band stretch** improves flexibility of the iliotibial band. Lie on your back with the left knee bent. Place the right ankle just above the left knee. While holding the foot steady with one arm, gently push the right leg straight forward until you feel the stretch.

upper back stretch

This **upper back stretch** improves flexibility of the upper back, lower back, and hip rotator. Starting from a seated position with the left leg extended forward, bend the right knee and put the right ankle over the left knee. Bring the left arm around the right knee and gently press against the right knee while gently turning the shoulders and trunk to the right. Perform on the opposite side.

REST, RECOVERY, AND SCHEDULING

A s fitness and training expert Jeff Drock points out, people can come back too soon before they are completely healed from injury, or they may be very nervous about an injury. Or they may come back too intensely and can injure other areas of the body. They may not be quite ready to play.

"Tennis differentiates from other sports; there's no off-season," he says. "Some players practice seven days a week. You need rest for the body and the mind to recover. Don't play every day. Take off a minimum of one day a week, preferably two. And limit practice days to approximately four hours of intense practice, minus any extraneous physical fitness/injury prevention program that a player may take part in, even at the highest levels.

"A main goal must be to keep healthy. In tennis this is especially true because competition is year-round and there is no scheduled offseason on the professional level and on the competitive junior level."

Once you have an injury, Drock emphasizes how difficult it is to take the time off.

"You can work on other parts of your game, such as feel, or drop shots. If it's an upper-body injury you can do core work.

"If it's a lower-body injury, work while sitting in a chair and work on strokes and volleys."

Satoshi Ochi notes that icing and heat are important for prevention and recovery of injuries:

"If it's an acute injury, usually it's the icing," Ochi says. "Use compresses for treatment. For the recovery purpose, ice or ice packs have been used for many years for the muscle tissues, not only the injury. We use the ice pack a lot, soaking [for] 10 minutes [at a time]."

Ochi explained that heating serves a variety of purposes. It is particularly helpful for the warm-up or if you want to address a tightness prior to your actual workout.

Ochi also sung the praises of contrast baths: "Contrast baths—[a] cold bath to warm bath—will help the circulation to the tissues at the same time you're doing icing. That's the two things I see a lot for injury and recovery."

When it comes to using Epson salts in your bath, though, Ochi said that the verdict is still not yet out: "It's more of a feel-good type of factor. I saw an article saying it's a placebo effect. At this point, if it works for you, use it."

Renowned coach and International Tennis Hall of Fame inductee Nick Bollettieri offers advice on recovering from an injury, regardless of the methods you apply:

"Rehabilitation takes commitment, hard work, perseverance, and most of all patience. Professional athletes are very familiar with all four of these character traits. What they are often not as familiar with is losing ground. They are always training to improve themselves, to get to the next level up, not to drop back and spend valuable time just trying to regain their health and their rank."

He points out that athletes expect a lot from their bodies and injuries are more than just a minor annoyance, they can be life changing. Every injury could end a career, leaving the player to face the next chapter in his or her life much sooner than planned.

Bollettieri, no doubt, speaks from experience: "Over my fifty-plus years in this sport I have seen many career-ending injuries. Every time a great athlete succumbs to such an injury the devastation is felt almost as intensely by their fans, their family, their coaches and staff, and in most cases by the entire tennis community, as it is by the athlete themselves."

His wife has told him she is certain that in his previous life he was a Jack Russell Terrier. At first that offended Bollettieri until someone explained that this breed is know for its tenacity and willingness to fight even when the opponent is a pit bull and all appears lost. So now he takes the comparison as a compliment and says it may also explain why he has such admiration for that kind of spirit in others. Families from all over the world visit Bollettieri's IMG Academy in Bradenton, Florida, to have him evaluate their child's potential on the tennis court. He emphasizes the importance of the child's resiliency in his evalutation.

"It is this gumption that not only will keep them fighting in an apparent losing battle, but will bode well for them should they ever face the dragon of injury."

Bollettieri cited the journey of James Blake, ranked number 30 in 2003, as an example of this gumption. "And, then in 2004 Murphy's Law reared its ugly head. While practicing in Rome with Robby Ginepri, Blake broke his neck when he slipped on the clay and collided with the net post. In July of that same year his father died of stomach cancer, which also coincided with James developing a serious case of shingles that temporarily paralyzed half of his face and blurred his vision. There is no one who would have blamed him for hanging it up and calling it quits. He dropped down to number 210 in the world and decided to play the Challenger circuit in order to regain his confidence. By the end of 2005, Blake was back up to number 23 in the world. He reached his career high rank of number 4 in the world in 2006, and remained in the top for several years, a true testament to his desire to stay in the game."

Bollettieri also sang the praises of Tommy Haas, who he knew since Haas was just thirteen years old. "Although his antics on court have gotten him a reputation as a hothead, I've always admired his fire and flair," Bollettieri said. "In fact, I believe it is this energy that got him through 2002 which he spent the majority of his time caring for his parents after they were in a devastating motorcycle accident that left them both in critical condition with his dad in a coma. Soon after returning to the game, Tommy seriously injured his shoulder. He endured surgeries and multiple rehabs and wouldn't return full-time to the game until 2004. He then climbed back into the top 10 in 2007, reaching number 9 in the world. Despite all of the hurdles he has faced, Tommy still has the best backhand and one of the shortest tempers on the tour; but, much more important is the confidence he gained from having tested and proven his warrior spirit in the face of adversity."

For Taylor Dent, it was three back surgeries for a fractured vertebra that kept him out of tennis for more than two years. Doctors told him that he had a 20 percent chance of returning to the court, yet those odds were good enough to keep him from giving up. "I was wracking my brain thinking of stuff I wanted to do, and honestly nothing gave me the fire in my belly like competing and playing professional tennis," Dent said. "So I said if I get the chance I'm going to take it, and I'm going to try to be better than I was." Dent returned to Bollettieri's Academy and trained full-time with no pain. "He worked as hard as anyone I have ever met to get back on the court and you could see on his face how happy he was to be playing again," Bollettieri said.

After Dent's ranking tumbled into the 800s, he came all the way back to number 76 and was a candidate for Comeback Player of the Year in 2009 before announcing his retirement in 2010.

On the women's side, Bollettieri admires Monica Seles, Mary Pierce, and Jennifer Capriati for their bounce-back abilities. "Monica Seles showed what she was really made of when her two-year ride as the number 1 player in the world came to a screeching halt when in a bizarre twist of fate she was stabbed in the back by a German spectator during a match against Steffi Graf. With the exception of just a few people, no one was sure if anyone could ever come back psychologically from this tragedy. Fortunately, one of the individuals who did have faith in her ability to come back was Monica herself. She came back in 1995 and reached the final of the US Open, where she lost to Steffi Graf. She went on the win the 1996 Australian Open and retired ranked number 2 in the world.

For Pierce, a comeback has been a long time in the making. "Mary Pierce tore the ACL in her left knee during a match in October, 2006. She underwent surgery and rehabilitation, but has yet to return to the tour." Pierce has stated that she still wants to return to tennis.

"Many people have asked me why Mary would want to come back at the age of thirty-four after having had such a great career," Bollettieri explained. "Knowing Mary as I do, it didn't surprise me one bit. Mary is a true professional who doesn't want to end her career being wheeled off on a stretcher; instead she wants to end it on her own terms."

Pierce recovered well enough to be named to the 2008 French tennis team in the Beijing Olympics but withdrew because of injury. "The fact that she has put so much effort into her rehab and practiced hard [means] Mary will be able to go through life with few regrets because she gave it her all," Bollettieri said.

In Capriati's case, it was surgery for a shoulder injury that kept her out of tennis beginning in 2005. Bollettieri explained, "I think Jennifer summed up the way many professional athletes feel when after two years and two additional surgeries she stated that she still wanted to come back because if she didn't have tennis then she feared she would lose her identity. She said in an interview with the New York *Daily News* in July 2007, 'When I stopped playing, that's when all this came crumbling down. If I don't have [tennis], who am I? What am I? I was just alive because of this. I've had to ask, Well, who is Jennifer? What if this is gone now?'"

Bollettieri believes these stories provide inspiration to anyone facing misfortune.

Focus on Junior Players

Rick Macci, who coached five players in their formative years who reached the number 1 ranking on the pro tour, believes rest, recovery, and scheduling "is really an important topic because a lot of times people think more is better. And people are chasing points, they're chasing tournaments, you want a better ranking. It's nonstop just to get as many tournaments in as possible.

Yet for kids, Macci emphasizes, this nonstop approach is not necessarily healthy: "Especially for kids it's very critical not to stunt their growth. They should get eight to ten hours of sleep at night. A lot of times parents have kids get up early, two hours before school, and even though they're getting in repetitions in practice it could have an impact on just how their kid is developing. It's just like a flower, you need the sun and water, you need to sleep and eat right. And a lot of parents lose sight of that. Even when a kid is twelve they're buying a ticket to Wimbledon already, and it doesn't work that way."

The key is balance. More is not better.

Macci believes that parents don't have the knowledge to understand that how a player eats has a profound affect on their mood and how they perform.

"A lot of parents do what they did as kids," he said. "The problem is they are not playing. They really need to get educated in this field of nutrition because a lot of kids eat a lot of sweets and sugar."

The guidance of parents and/or guardians is also important in helping juniors respond to adversity on the court. Wayne Bryan, respected long-time coach in Southern California and father of the most prolific men's doubles team in professional tennis history, writes about bouncing back after disappointments in his book *Raising Your Child to be a Champion in Athletics, Arts, and Academics.* Bryan says he can recall times when his sons Mike and Bob suffered a tough loss on the tennis court.

"For those super tough losses and really big disappointments, however, the recovery time may be perhaps a few days," Bryan said. "Perhaps even a week or until the next contest. After a tough loss, Mike and Bob could never wait until their next match ... Instead of brooding over what just happened, it puts their mind on what's coming up next.

"It's impossible for a kid who has been on the planet for 8 or 10 or 12 years to have the perspective that you do after being here for 25 or 30 or 50 years," Bryan writes. "It is your role to share your experiences and perspective. You do this through both your words and your deeds."

Bryan encourages parents not to get down on themselves because their child will feed off this. If you are upbeat and positive during the trying times, your child will get through this period easier and quicker. He points out that kids are resilient and recover quickly "if we just back off a little and let them. Indeed, one of the worst things you can do is to smother your child with sympathy after a loss or disappointment. It's far better to let kids hang around with their friends."

Another way to show perspective to a child, Bryan said, is to ask him/her what they think makes tennis great. And help them with the answers. For example: "I personally think tennis is great because you can play it your entire lifetime, size does not matter, boys and girls can play together, it is great exercise, you can make friends," and so on.

Keys to Tournament Scheduling

Lorenzo Beltrame, the Director of Athletic Performance Coaching and Director of Tennis at the Johnson & Johnson Human Performance Institute in Orlando, notes that designing a strategic tournament schedule is a vital skill that players need to develop if they want to achieve the success they desire. In his experience, too many players make critical mistakes in choosing their tournaments and, by doing so, compromise their chances of achieving their dreams.

Here are some recommendations from Beltrame on how to map out your tournament schedule:

- First, establish your long-term goals. If you wish to play professional tennis, be aware that there are some high expenses that you have to incur as you start playing on the tour. At Futures and Challengers level, the prize money may not cover the expenses of traveling, lodging, coaching, etc. If you wish to earn a college scholarship, you will want to get good exposure and a good national ranking at the age of sixteen or seventeen. Bottom line: He believes that if you don't have unlimited financial funds, don't waste all your money playing in the ten-year-old, twelve-year-old, and fourteen-year-old divisions. These categories are important to gain a competitive experience and to gauge your improvements against players of similar age, but the ranking you achieve there will mean very little in the big picture. His recommendation for those years is to play enough tournaments to make sure that your ranking allows you to compete among the best players in your category.

- Second, Beltrame highly recommends that you establish short-term goals. Challenge yourself to achieve a level of competition higher than the one you are currently competing in, and choose a particular tournament that you would like to play in the future. For example, if you are a sectional player, try to achieve a ranking that allows you to play nationals and choose a particular national tournament as your objective. Design a schedule that provides you with enough chances to build the points you need to achieve the ranking required to play in that special tournament. Do not play tournaments that are not in line with your goal. Save your time, energy, and money for when you really need it. Other examples of short-term goals include, if you're a national player, for example, a desire to compete for an international level, or you're a player who plays mainly in Futures or Challengers, a desire to compete in ATP/WTA Tour tournaments and, ultimately, in the Grand Slams.

- Finally, don't forget to schedule periods of training, rest, and vacation. Everybody needs them.

A smart schedule is a key factor for successful players. Learn to design yours to enhance your chances for success.

Renowned tennis coach, researcher, psychologist, and author, the late Vic Braden, wrote in a column for *Florida Tennis Magazine* about the importance of scheduling matches in the proper age group. He referenced an article in the Los Angeles Times on Aug. 22, 1983, under the headline: "Reality Sets in for Martin, Sampras."

The article was about the Disney National Junior Tennis Championships at the Vic Braden Tennis College in California, and it focused on unseeded Stacey Martin of Largo, Maryland, and underaged, undersized Pete Sampras of Rancho Palos Verdes, California. Regarding Sampras, the article said; "The five-foot, 83-pound Sampras, who celebrated his 12th birthday just last week, was a finalist in the boys' 14-and-under division, despite being at an age, weight and height disadvantage against virtually every opponent he faced."

In the final, a tired Sampras, after playing four matches in two days, fell quickly to third-seeded Nicholas Barone of Des Plaines, Illinois, 6-1, 6-1. As the article noted, tennis followers know what happened to Pete, but only a few know whatever happened to Nicholas Barone.

Richard Williams, the father of Venus and Serena, kept his girls out of junior competition. The Bryan twins, Bob and Mike, played up one level because there was no competition for them in their own age division. Underaged Donald Young took beatings in the pro ranks eleven times in a row but later made a significant move up the professional ladder. Braden recalls that Ken Rosewall and Lew Hoad joined the pro ranks at a very early age and became tennis leaders in the 1960s and early 1970s.

"It all sounds wonderful, but I know situations where children played up one age level and seldom won a match and quit tennis at an early age," Braden said. "As a psychologist, I prefer to look at the personality and game of each person who wants to play up. Taking twenty to thirty beatings in a row doesn't do much for one's ego."

Sometimes players will play up because they don't want to lose to someone in their own age bracket. And some players are convinced there will be a glory day at the end of the experiment. But as Braden noted, it seems to happen only to a select few. "We need to know why a youngster wants to play up. Is there rationale to support their wish? Can the player handle continued losses? Is there a quantifiable gain in playing ability? Is one playing up because of wishes of the coach, or parent?"

Braden recognized that a player would want to play up if he/she had no competition in their age bracket. Tracy Austin, for instance, never lost a match in her own age division, and she won the US National Championships at age 17.

"I personally think there's a lot to learning to beat people in one's age bracket. The pressure is greater in this scenario than being able to say, 'I lost, but I was playing up one level.'"

Braden concluded by saying the college experience helps one learn to play under pressure and provides backup when one is definitely never going to make it in the pro ranks.

Training After the Holidays

Put on a few extra pounds during the holidays? This excess weight will not only slow you down on the court but will also put extra stress on your feet, knees, and back.

Renowned fitness coach Pat Etcheberry says the best way for him to show people how much of a difference excess weight makes on the court is to have a player put on a weighted jacket or a weight plate in their shorts. The weight is equal to the amount that the player is overweight. "Then I tell them to try to play tennis," he said. "Right away the player will tell me that they can't move and they get tired very quickly."

A player once asked Etcheberry for his help to get ready for the pro tour. He was a good player, but his body fat percentage was 17.5. That is way too high for someone wanting to compete on the men's tour.

"I told him that for instance Pete Sampras would not have reached the top 50 and maybe not even the top 100 in the world at a body fat percentage of 17.5," Etcheberry said. "Most of the top players on the men's tour range from 8 to 10 percent body fat."

He noted that if you want to drop the pounds you added during the holidays, add more cardio training to your routine but still do some strength training so that when you lose weight you will lose fat tissue and not muscle tissue. Also look at your eating habits and clean up your diet. Reduce the amount of processed foods that you eat. Also, make sure you eat breakfast every day.

Set up realistic goals as to how much weight you want to lose each week. One pound a week is a good goal. If you lose the weight slowly you are more likely to keep the pounds off.

For your cardio routine, Etcheberry recommends finding the form of cardio that you most enjoy. This way you are more likely to stick with your program. Good cardio choices include walking, jogging, biking, swimming, and elliptical machine.

Sleep Well and Perform Well

If you don't have regular sleeping habits, or simply don't get enough sleep, that probably will affect your performance on the tennis court. And that can hinder you physically and mentally. Chris Jordan says "a lack of sleep can seriously compromise brain function and can affect you both emotionally and mentally. After a night with little or no sleep, typically, you will feel physically tired, but also irritable, impatient, and moody. In addition, sleep deprivation can compromise your memory and planning skills, as well as your sense of time. Furthermore, sleep-deprived individuals find it difficult to respond to rapidly changing situations and making rational decisions.

"As a tennis player, wouldn't you prefer to feel physically energized, positive, focused, and prepared for anything before a game, instead of tired, moody and prone to making errors? The bottom line is simple. You must sleep well to perform well in anything that matters to you."

Jordan adds, "Sleep is a physiological condition of the body where many of the bodily functions are maintained at a minimum level of energy expenditure. Sleep occurs in stages. The first, [which lasts for] approximately ten minutes, is light sleep, then true sleep (approximately twenty minutes) followed by deep sleep (approximately thirty to sixty minutes) and finally REM sleep. Then this cycle repeats. If you cannot get to sleep or if this sequence is disrupted, sleep deprivation and reduced physical and mental performance can result."

Jordan recommends the following in order to maximize the benefits that one receives from a solid sleep:

- Go to bed and wake up at the same time every day to develop a sleep/awake rhythm.
- Aim to get seven to eight hours a night; however, the more fit you are the less sleep you may need.
- Create a bedtime ritual, such as getting undressed, brushing your teeth, and then reading a book, to send a signal to the brain that it is time to sleep.
- Make sure your bedroom temperature is cool and your mattress is not too soft.
- Avoid drinks or foods that contain caffeine such as tea, coffee, sodas, and chocolate, just before going to bed. Caffeine is a stimulant and can disrupt your sleep cycles. Nicotine is a stimulant and should be avoided, too. Alcohol may put you to sleep, but its effects wear off and can ultimately disrupt your sleep cycles.
- Exercise in the late afternoon may invigorate you for two to three hours and then help you sleep. If you do awake during the night and cannot get to sleep within thirty minutes, get up and do something boring to help you switch off.

- Avoid watching television in bed and turning your bedroom into an entertainment center.
- Dimming the lights will send a signal to the brain that it is time to sleep. If you still have trouble, try a few deep breathing exercises to slow your metabolism, relax the muscles, clear your mind, and gradually drift into sleep.

CHAPTER 7

PAIN OF FEAR, LOSS, AND CHOKING

T he mental side of tennis was long overlooked, but in recent years it has become a crucial component of training and development. Fear and choking are part of tennis at every level of the sport. Moreover, an injury can affect your mental stability.

Chris Evert, professional tennis legend and now a television commentator and coach at her academy in Florida, explains how she learned to play without fear: "My father taught me one important lesson: not to be afraid to lose." And the late noted coach, researcher, and author Vic Braden said, "Basically, the reason you choke is that you don't have the strokes."

Satoshi Ochi notes there is a full-time mental skills professional on the staff of the USTA, Dr. Larry Lauer, "and he and I communicate a lot. We work as a team because we use the mental toughness or the mental skills training throughout the training. In some of the mental skills training they are working a lot on breathing techniques that simulate the on-court performance. So that after a tough long point, it's a matter of how quickly you can come down and get in the right mental state. We practice that during the fitness training."

Dr. Robert S. Weinberg, a professor of physical education, health, and sports studies at Miami University in Ohio and an internationally respected author, says, "there really is not anything out there on using mental strategies to avoid injury other than some research on how increased stress can cause inappropriate focus of attention which could lead to an injury. For example, if you are stressed out because of something outside of the game (e.g., you broke up with a girlfriend or boyfriend) and your mind was not on the game, then you might NOT be paying attention to your positioning or opponent, which could result in injury.

"There is more written about the use of MENTAL strategies (e.g., goal-setting, imagery, relaxation) to help athletes recover quicker from injury."

Weinberg says the term "mental injuries" is not appropriate, although mental processes (e.g., stress and attention) could potentially make it more likely that one could get injured.

Frank Giampaolo, a Southern California–based tennis coach, researcher, and instructional writer who founded The Tennis Parents Workshop in 1998, writes in his book *The Tennis Parent's Bible* that poor physical fitness manifests in mental and emotional breakdowns. "For instance, most juniors go for low percentage shots due to the fact that they are too tired to grind out the point. So is off-court training linked to the mental side? Absolutely!"

Giampaolo believes proper hydration and nutrition is also a critical factor in the physical, mental, and emotional links of every tennis competitor. "As parents, we have to insist that our players fuel up before battle. Dehydration triggers fatigue, dizziness, headaches and nausea. Improper nutrition lowers the blood sugar levels to the brain. Improper nutrition and hydration guarantees poor decision-making skills at crunch time."

Injury Affecting Mental Stability

Research has long established that physical health is directly connected to mental and emotional health. Dr. John F. Murray, a Florida-based sports psychologist and clinical psychologist who works with many tennis players and athletes in other sports, believes that avoiding injury and staying healthy fall within the area of well-being or health, "and we know from infinite studies that a sound and healthy mind and mind-set, or mental skills, or mental performance, whatever you want to call it, feeds a sense of physical health and well-being, and that when things are not going well physically, such as in an injury, mental stability can often suffer.

"Another aspect is that injuries and pain are often very subjective and medical doctors often bring in a psychologist because even with the best pain assessments available, many doctors are often at a loss to help their patients because pain is such a subjective experience. And not only that, individuals have greatly different pain tolerance levels. You also frequently see that people who have experienced trauma of some sort (ranging from A–Z and can include physical or emotional trauma, sports injuries, unresolved conflicts from the past, etc.) often experience greater and more pervasive pain. What this all elicits too is the need to cope with pain and injury better.

"A person can be fine physically and a mess mentally, and we know from many stories and case studies that emotional and mental distress or unhappiness is much more devastating than a broken leg or sprained ankle. So, for example, many billionaires are unhappy and depressed, and perfectionism prevents you from enjoying your physical well-being, your wins, and your progress, to the extent that you often become a nasty, ugly, and self-loathing person who is no fun to be around.

"I think you can realize how huge this is, the importance of mental factors for health and well-being, and how the mental side is often given short shrift due simply to ignorance or bias or lack of qualified providers.

"And I think it's also fairly clear that seventeenth century French philosopher Descartes, as smart as he was, made a huge mistake to separate the mind and body historically and led many good people to make faulty assumptions about health that unnecessarily excluded the many mental aspects. It would have been better if early physicians and philosophers had realized what we have learned and realized in the past sixty years, namely that we are all one, not some divided mind-body dualistic entity who must fight with himself or herself. Stated simply, we must consider the person as a whole; mind and body are inseparable. Mind affects body as much as body affects mind."

Murray tried to use that approach in writing the book *Smart Tennis* and coming up with the metric of four modes of expression: thoughts, feelings, sensations, and actions, so that he could capture a more fully human experience without buying into the nonsense perpetuated by Descartes and purchased by the strict and limited traditional medical community.

In his most recent book, *The Mental Performance Index*, he writes about the vitality and importance of the mind and mental skills and how we ignore them always to our detriment.

Murray notes that injuries have been described as the greatest source of stress and the single-most important issue in sports. They may lead to emotional problems such as anxiety and depression, and unhealthy behaviors such as increased drug and alcohol abuse. These negative moods and behaviors place the athlete at risk for prolonged rehabilitation and further behavioral problems.

There are an estimated seventeen million annual sport injuries in the United States alone, but surprisingly little research has examined the consequence of sport injury or psychological factors which may promote healing. For example, why do some athletes adjust to injuries with increased optimism and effort, while others with even less severe physical damage plunge into the depths of depression or fail to comply with treatment recommendations? These types of questions prompted Murray to pursue this topic for his dissertation at the University of Florida.

Although more severe injuries obviously occur in contact sports such as football and boxing, injured tennis players may also endure great distress from any number of losses including lost playing time, forfeited scholarships, decreased self-esteem, or simply the lack of a pleasurable outlet.

Sport psychologists are becoming fully integrated members of the world's best sports medicine teams and are involved in all aspects of athlete care including injury prevention, assessment, and rehabilitation. Whether you have access to a sport psychologist or not, the following are some tips from Murray to help you, or those close to you, in coping with a difficult injury in tennis or other sports. Keep in mind that these tips are never a substitute for qualified professional care:

- Maintain a positive, yet realistic, attitude about injury diagnosis and treatment options.
- Make sincere efforts to understand how the athlete interprets the meaning of the injury, avoiding careless assumptions. This knowledge defines the scope of the loss, and sincere empathy goes a long way toward recovery.
- Social support protects against many negative effects of stress. The athlete should stay in touch with friends, family, and teammates on a regular basis.
- Successful performance imagery should be used to keep skills and strategies sharp, even when real practice is impossible. Regular imagery can also be targeted to help defeat the fear of re-injury.
- Difficult yet attainable short- and long-term goals should be set to monitor progress and speed recovery.
- Seek professional therapy when severe psychological distress is suspected (e.g., depression or severe anxiety).

The Pain of Loss

Dr. Allen Fox, who two decades ago wrote one of the first books about the strategy and mental dimension of the sport, is an acclaimed California-based coach, sports psychologist, and author. In his more recent book *The Winner's Mind* he writes about when losing hurts the most and points out that that the harder you try to win, and the more you invest emotionally, the greater the pain of loss.

"Winning and losing tennis matches strikes an immediate and resonant emotional chord because it is an individual sport, and the loser walks off the court with his status directly and painfully diminished relative to the victor," Fox says. "Here the emotional responses of the loser are amplified because the underlying nature of a tennis match is a symbolic fight for superiority and there is a genetic contribution to the fear of failure and the potential pain of loss. For this reason, it is painful to lose almost any tennis match in which one invests a reasonable amount of effort, even if it is just a Sunday afternoon recreational match played solely (supposedly) for exercise and fun."

Fox says that when he lost a tournament match, he was in agony, sometimes for days. Right after losing he didn't want to talk to anyone and felt like hiding in his room, locking the door, and never coming out. "No one taught me to feel this way, but it was my invariable and instinctive reaction," he says. "I suffered great pain because my investment in winning was total. I was not a great athlete, but I was a perfectionist and did everything possible to improve my chances of winning. I practiced endless hours, concentrated with ferocious intensity, and never gave up, regardless of the score or situation. And when I went down, I went down hard. I sound silly admitting this, but even losing a practice match was enough to ruin my day."

Fox believes that fear is also learned, saying, "Pain causes fear, and anyone who has competed hard and lost knows that losing is painful."

In regard to a player's reaction to failure, Fox says, "The champion reacts to failure with increased determination to succeed rather than discouragement. When tennis champions lose a match, their instincts are to go to the practice court, work harder, and improve, while those with loser mentalities become disheartened and less inclined to practice. Losses simply motivate the champions to get better. They will assess their weaknesses and strive to fix them. They will get into better physical condition and work to hone their weapons so that the next time they enter the arena they will be better armed."

Fox insists that the drive of champions to control their fate impels them to take action. They know that if they do nothing the losses will continue, and they are not willing to let that happen. The losers, on the other hand, weaken and do little, if anything, to save themselves from additional failures.

"You can see that if the champion's approach is applied consistently over time, it will eventually produce a very good tennis player," Fox says. "In like manner, setbacks drive the winner business people to seek, work on, and fix the causes of their setbacks. They are stimulated to additional effort. They think about their problems, turn them over thoroughly in their minds, and develop plans for productive changes. The losers are disheartened and inclined toward escape rather than investing more work."

Choke Busting

Murray believes that there are many talented tennis players who attend the finest academies, are well-conditioned physically, and love their sport. Unfortunately, they often unravel and choke just when they are on the verge of making a real breakthrough. Coaches, parents, and even the players themselves are befuddled about why their performance falters after they gain a seemingly decisive lead in the final set of the big tournament.

The answer to this challenge is frequently found in sports psychology and mental skills training, Murray says. Dealing with competitive pressure is never easy, but it is an important part of the game. These players are rarely disturbed in the clinical sense until after their fifth major choke. "Rather, they are responding naturally to a highly unnatural situation mentally," Murray says. "It's not easy to stare at a major victory (or defeat) and calmly ignore it. Thoughts become scrambled, muscles tighten, and the heart pounds and the ball keeps flying into the net. Meanwhile, the opponent with nothing to lose plays fierce tennis and finds himself or herself a happy winner."

The origin of the choke lies within the processes of attention control and energy regulation, Murray notes. In sport psychology sessions, players begin to see that their problem is universal. They gradually realize that the "pressure" of the moment is a greater adversary than any opponent. They also learn that choking can never be completely extinguished because competitors care about winning, care about what others think, and want to improve. However, they gradually learn to change their thoughts about what it means to be a strong tennis player and begin putting self-awareness and thought control into action. After learning to master this huge challenge, they wonder why they never practiced "choke-busting" long ago. Since practice situations rarely simulate the excitement or pressure of the big match, players must patiently monitor their feelings, evaluate performance in a slightly different way, love the struggles, and go for it with confidence and courage even in the scariest moments.

Former ATP Tour player Vince Spadea had the longest losing streak in pro tennis history—21 matches. He overcame it, though, and noted the role that his sport psychology sessions with Murray had in his comeback.

So, how you can reverse your own losing streak?

"Attitude is key," Murray says. "Nobody enjoys losing. Even more confounding is to lose repeatedly over a long period of time. Before long, this pattern takes on a life all its own, becoming an even greater foe than the person on the other side of the net."

As former WTA Tour star and ESPN tennis analyst Lindsay Davenport said, "the game with yourself is often tougher than the battle against any opponent."

Rather than just playing tennis, players on a losing streak often dwell too long on their results and begin to perceive themselves as being trapped or stuck, Murray points out.

Trying too hard to pull out of the slump makes it even worse, as the player's mental skills are often severely disrupted, he adds. For example, he sees people losing confidence (even though this is can be controlled), becoming overly intense, focusing on irrelevant thought, and setting totally inappropriate goals. The bottom line is that the momentum of losing often leads to a distress of its own, and this continues the pattern of losing. It's a vicious cycle of negativity.

Why does this slump happen? There are many possible answers to this question, Murray says. Competition is very delicate and complex, and momentum plays a huge role. It may be that a player simply lost to a better opponent six times in a row and he/she is deluded into thinking that they should have won each match. Then when they actually should win, they lose. Momentum takes over.

"Expectations have a great impact on performance too," Murray adds. "Just as it helps to remain confident, always expecting the best, the reverse holds true too. Expecting the worst usually gets you there. Negative self-talk leads to negative performance and results. The mind cannot stay focused on the bad and the good at the same time.

"The equilibrium that is disrupted by trying too hard to over-compensate, or giving up out of despair, must also be considered. Athletes need to remain optimally focused and energized. Too much fluctuation to any direction over a short period of time leads to lapses in attention and problems with consistency. It's hard enough to play a solid tennis match without having mental skills disrupted too. Throw in the inner turmoil caused by frustration and you have a tangled mess."

Another problem is being distracted by off-court issues.

Murray offers seven steps to dig yourself out of a slump. He says the first thing to do is take a break, short or long, from tennis. This might be a weekend-long outing or one that lasts several months, depending upon your situation and needs. Do anything to leave the performance situation for awhile and calmly approach a solution. Nothing can be accomplished if you do not first reduce the intensity, change the scenery, and reflect.

After finding the time and place to do some repair work, here are some specific tips from Murray to follow:

1. While in a calm state, spend thirty minutes taking a complete inventory of why you love tennis. If you cannot find any positives, you are ready for a much longer break from your sport.
2. Tell yourself that for the next three months after you begin again you will simply play for the reasons you listed in number one.
3. Find other physical activities to go along with your tennis. For example, play basketball a couple hours each week, or take up softball once a week. This type of cross-training will help recharge your tennis batteries.

4. Begin to focus on a completely different aspect of performance. For example, take a look at your focus, independent of how well you are hitting the ball or whether you are winning or losing. You might, for example, make a goal to improve your focus over the next two weeks. Rate how focused you were throughout your match on a 1–10 scale. Each time you perform, you try to raise the level of your focus. By the end of two weeks, you have achieved success in mental skills development if you can consistently hit a 9 or 10 in focus. This is completely within your control, as opposed to a match result, which is not. Your focus is on focus, not on outcome.

5. Change your training routine, develop new strategy. The main thing is to inject freshness into your tennis. Change clothing, grip tape, or shoes. These minor adjustments often contribute to renewed enjoyment of the sport.

6. Take all the pressure off by forgetting about winning and losing for awhile. Set goals to perform better rather than to win or lose. Change your focus to skills and effort, while letting the outcome take care of itself.

7. If none of these tips work after a couple of months, give serious thoughts to sport psychology counseling. This never indicates weakness. This is simply a search for excellence and many do it before problems even come up.

Murray argues that much of our behavior is habit and momentum. It's often just as difficult to change a winning streak as it is to change losing. A losing streak is not rare. It's just a time to take stock, refresh batteries, and see the picture from a slightly different angle. In time, you'll be back enjoying the competition as much as the victories.

Stop Doubting: Attitude of a Beginner's Mind

Talent, effort, and mental skills—when you ace all three areas, you have a superb chance of winning. You need to remember, however, that winning is only guaranteed if the opponent cooperates. You might score high in all three areas and play the best match of your life but still lose. So while high performance may be realized, it never really guarantees a victory. It only increases the probability.

In providing sport psychology services to athletes at many levels, Murray has found that one particular mindset is useful in unlocking true potential in a person. It is the attitude of the beginner's mind—open and trusting—that seems to work well. No matter how accomplished an athlete may be or how much he or she knows, an innocence and almost naive trust in your plan together is what sets the stage for learning and excellence. He calls this attitude "belief."

Murray distinguishes between the role of belief in the world of sports versus its lesser importance in areas like science.

"We sent men to the moon and discovered the cures for diseases not by believing, but by doubting and analyzing and thinking in an extremely critical manner," he says. "This form of healthy doubt is the hallmark of the scientific revolution and serves us well in creating knowledge, but doubt in an athlete's mind always sidetracks progress and sabotages performance."

The problem with doubt for an athlete is that an awful lot of energy and left-brain thinking is required to analyze critically and consider the possibilities of behavior, Murray says. Doubt disrupts flow and focus and reduces confidence. To perform with grace and efficiency on the tennis court requires an almost single-minded trust in the chosen method.

"In working with an athlete, whether as coach or sport psychologist, it's essential to establish trust and explain the benefits that occur with simple belief," Murray adds. "Not every word out of a good mentor's mouth needs to be founded on empirical evidence. Far from it. A good part of any coaching and counseling is art, based upon intuition, smart risks, trends, and hunches.

"It is often the athlete's basic and simple belief that produces a more refined and advanced state. Much has been written about the placebo effect in which sugar pills cure pain as effectively as Tylenol. The mechanism of action is simple caveman-like belief. This placebo effect is just as critical in getting an athlete ready for peak performance.

Following are some guidelines offered by Murray in helping promote basic belief. Whether you are an athlete, coach, sports psychologist, or highly involved tennis parent, you will find these useful:

1. Whatever you are doing, make sure that your approach is based on sound principles. Although belief is important, belief alone never suffices. Establish trust by showing that what you are doing is credible.
2. Paint a total picture for the athlete. Show that person what it takes to achieve high performance and how goals will be accomplished. Only after showing the grand scheme is it time to address details.
3. Simplify your message. Rather than trying to accomplish everything at once, target one skill at a time until mastery occurs. Confusion destroys belief and performance.
4. Never promise victory, but always promise higher performance. Control over outcome is a myth. False promises reduce belief.

With solid knowledge and total belief in place, the athlete is more confident, freed from doubts, and allowed to express their inner caveman, Murray says. Focus on basic belief as much as skills and you'll release the inner beast from captivity.

In his book *The Mental Performance Index*, Murray notes that we get a dental check-up twice a year without thinking about it, and a haircut at least six times a year, but people tend to go for mental help only when things get beyond repair or quite out of control. He raises this question: Are your hair and teeth far more important than your success on the field or your entire well-being? "There should never be shame in going to talk with someone who can help, if nothing more than to get better," he says.

Murray believes that it is an indication of health and strength when you face a problem and defeat it directly rather than let it fester and affect you worse. He notes that athletes at all levels are just people, and people need to be watched and cared for. And he suggests that sometimes people take care of their plants, cars, and dogs better than they do people themselves. He believes that has to change.

If an athlete has a problem, he or she needs to be able to get help and quickly, and not run into the trap of thinking that talking is a sign of weakness," he says in his book. "The additional expertise in sports psychology/mental coaching provides an easy way to talk with an athlete who is raised in a sports culture that may not easily encourage verbal openness. By keeping it initially to discussions about performance or the upcoming game (or tennis match), it really helps ease the transition to other more serious issues when they come up. But I don't want to give the impression either that this is just for off-field issues. I work with a variety of athletes in all sports and also a variety of business situations in which the focus has nothing to do with general well-being and we spend the session strategizing for improved performance. Again it depends on the individual and what the person needs."

The Role of Fear

Fear is often a paralyzing force when students are on the brink of a major breakthrough in tennis performance, Braden said. Coaches have experienced this phenomenon for years: A student begins to accept a small change during the lesson and then reverts right back to the old style of play one hour later in a match.

What's happening?

"There are many reasons given by experts, but for me there is some pain that goes with change," Braden said. "If the pain one suffers in making a change is greater than the pain one suffers in losing to people, there will probably never be the desired change. On the other hand, if the pain of losing is greater than the pain one might suffer in making a change, the prognosis is normally great. So how do expert coaches deal with pain, or the fear of changing?"

First, Braden pointed out, we must look at the motor program one's brain has developed to handle stroke production and strategy. One's brain becomes comfortable with the status quo, and for most people the brain will stick with comfort over affecting needed changes. To support this theory, Braden said, why is it that the majority of tennis players stay in their same playing level for decades?

Consider the typical club roster. Braden believed that when staging tournaments, it's easy to find sixty long-time veterans, year after year, competing in the 3.0 level. It's normally difficult to find enough 4.5 to 5.0 players to have a sixteen-player draw. If players have taken lessons year after year, shouldn't that scenario be reversed?

When Braden had tennis colleges in Germany, Switzerland, and Spain, he said he could go back year after year and see the same people playing exactly the same way they played the previous year. But the students who were willing to make the necessary changes were rapidly moving up the ladder. That was because the ladder was quite easily scaled due to the fact that most people did everything possible to stay on the same level.

"I have written about the role of coaches who hang onto students who are dedicated to making no changes," Braden said. "That's okay if the student is interested in paying good money to stay the same. Most professional coaches feel an obligation to end the relationship with students who are too afraid to change."

So what is this mysterious fear of changing? The anecdotal stories from students fall into hundreds of categories, but here are a few responses Braden gathered:

1. If I change, I could get worse.
2. If I change, I might lose my strengths.
3. Strangely, if I win, I might have to move up the ladder and take a lot of losses.
4. If I change, I might not have as much fun.
5. I don't like the feeling that goes with change.

6. I thought I at least had a little going for me, but when I tried to change, I lost everything.

First, Braden noted, it's important for coaches to study the human brain and emotions in order to understand each student's resistance to change. It's just as important to explain that one's brain does often get confused in giving up one comfortable motor program to accept a new, and often uncomfortable, motor program. When a student understands the brain's natural reluctance to change, the student is normally less fearful of facing the "changing period." When a student understands that there will possibly be a period of worsening performance and that even great players experience that sensation, it tends to reduce fear. When a student understands the logic of the need to change as well as the feelings that go with "change," and the key people around him/her are supportive, that same student can picture the improved performance levels of the future.

MENTAL WELL-BEING

M urray describes tennis as "chess on wheels" because it completely taxes your mental/strategic prowess while demanding extraordinary mobility and coordination. He offers eight tips to develop a tennis player's "high" and sharpen their skills:

1. Develop the confidence of a Grand Slam winner.
2. Stay properly focused during practice and match play.
3. Set and achieve appropriate tennis goals.
4. Keep your passion and joy for tennis alive.
5. Use imagery to your advantage.
6. Monitor and control your intensity levels.
7. Always word hard and smart.
8. Stay flexible and bounce back from losses quickly.

Playing tennis is its own reward, he says. You are playing one of the most wonderful physical and mental activities ever invented. Challenging yourself is the key.

The huge benefits of sport and exercise have been well documented. A special effect often talked about is called runner's high, which can be described as a sudden unexpected sensation, increased satisfaction, connection with nature, and perception of power. Murray argues that a tennis player's high is even higher because you are not only physically engaged, but you are challenging all your mental capacities as well in a fierce and fun battle.

Get addicted to this natural high and often, Murray says. There are so many benefits of playing tennis. It improves mental and emotional health, makes behavior more efficient, and enhances physical functioning and coordination.

Surroundings Make a Difference

Martina Hingis used to frown a lot when she competed on the WTA Tour, but upon her return to the circuit post-retirement, fans were seeing more smiles from this talented athlete. She was successful before retiring and upon her return to the tour. What was different?

"It's a lot more fun playing when the fans are behind you," she said.

The crowd loved having her different playing style back on the tour and they let her know it.

So what happens to the human brain when a player feels support rather than wrath? Braden noted that the front of the brain is where the best decisions are made, and one tends to use the front of the brain when not being threatened. It's easy to get to the less efficient back of the brain in competition, especially when one feels she/he has to beat the opponent and the crowd.

Since there is no such thing as muscle memory, Braden said, the brain has to feel comfortable to stay in the front while making critical decisions. The brain has to send down clear and appropriate messages to the muscles to affect winning strokes. We've seen players who are angry or scared, and they normally fold in competition.

Braden maintained that only a handful of professional players he knew in his sixty years of coaching were able to use anger as a meaningful motivator.

The worst case he saw involved hysterical paralysis when a golfer, having a ton of money riding on his next drive, completely froze and couldn't bring the golf club down from his shoulders to strike the ball. But he also saw tennis players down a match point who could barely get the ball out of their hands for the service toss.

"Even changes in stadium decor can wreck a person's brain," Braden said. "One year the research team at Michigan State University conducted an interesting study to determine why teams function better on their home court.

"Fan support was obvious, but there was another component that captured my attention. The researchers changed the ceiling banner arrangement, and the basketball court appeared strange to the players. Some remarked that it felt weird playing, but they weren't sure why. It's clear that we use familiarity to help us comfort our brain. And we use those familiar scenes as guides more than we realize."

One tennis player told Braden he was very successful returning his opponent's cross-court shot to successful down-the-line winners because all he had to do was to aim for the edge of one of the painted signs on the backdrop.

Obviously, the sign was geometrically positioned to allow for the right calculation to change the direction of the ball flight.

That means the French players have an edge at Roland Garros. And the competitors from Spain, who play on similar conditions day after day, should do well in Paris. And they usually do.

The bottom line, Braden pointed out, is that most players have discovered that it's wise to arrive one week earlier than the tournament starting date to allow their brain to become familiar with the surface and the surroundings.

Half the Players Competing Today Will Lose

Of those tennis players competing today, 50 percent will lose. The statistics seldom change. But that means 50 percent will win. However, Braden believes, the key to enjoying tennis for a lifetime is to learn how to enjoy this great game regardless of which half you find yourself in at the end of the day.

In a competitive field of sixty-four players in a tournament, sixty-three will lose. So learning to lose graciously while having fun is the challenge that adults, children, and coaches face, Braden noted. Ironically, the evidence seems to indicate we have a long way to go in this category.

"Unless we've been cheated out of a match, the reason we lose is that we're not as good as the other player on that particular day," Braden said.

When he mingled with players, parents, and children, he often heard a myriad of excuses, such as, "That bum hit a lucky shot," or "I just didn't feel like attacking the net today," or "I had him cold and I got a bad break."

Here's what he seldom heard: "Gee, he was just too tough today," or "She served so well under pressure," or "He is really just a better player than me."

Braden wondered why is it that many of us have trouble saying nice things about people who beat us.

"For one thing, people have a tendency to think that their self worth is threatened with such an admission," he said. "However, I have found that the greatest champions I know have been those who have a realistic viewpoint as to why they lost and thus have a realistic approach to solving the problem. People who blame losses on bad luck and other excuses are denying the fact that they have just experienced a loss that should have provided them with a checklist for the next few practice sessions. Plus, one's self-esteem is normally enhanced when one can honestly congratulate their victor."

In tennis, one has to come face to face with a term called "accountability," Braden noted, adding that you have earned your position in the tennis world. If you are the last on the ladder at your club or facility, it's because you are the worst player. That doesn't make you one degree less of a person. Someone has to be in last place, but fortunately you can do something about it. That's the beauty of tennis. Everyone can improve.

Braden worked with people who had suffered brain damage and they found some way to improve. He taught blind children to hit balls coming from a ball machine, and they improved. He watched quadriplegics learn how to guide a motorized chair with their mouth and hit tennis balls with a racquet taped to their arm, and they improved.

"All good coaches have watched hard-working students go from guaranteed losers to almost always winners," Braden said. "But you don't get good strokes and strategy in a lottery. You get them by intelligent thinking off the court and hard work on the court."

Some players simply don't improve. A woman once told Braden that she had no interest in improving her game. She said she only played one person, played her at the same time and on the same court each week, and normally beat her badly.

"The only tennis problem this person will have is when her opponent dies," Braden said. "For the rest of us, we generally want to improve our game so that we can move up a notch."

What keeps some people from improving? Most learning specialists spend a great deal of time studying how the human learns a sports skill, Braden pointed out. It's not as simple as one might think. First, one must understand that the muscle has no memory and so we have to focus on the human brain. That means one must have a clear understanding of what is fact or fiction in instruction.

"The brain must send complicated electrical messages down to the muscles," Braden said. "These electrical messages will be honored by the muscles, so they had better be right. If they're wrong, a person can play perfectly lousy each day. The adage of simply hitting thousands of tennis balls will eventually cure all problems has been proved to be a myth."

Braden believed the first order of business is to secure intelligent and truthful information, and that's not always available. There are thousands of dedicated and intelligent tennis pros who study the data presented by sports researchers around the world. But at the same time there are professionals who have no interest in research because they feel they already know what's best for each student.

In this scenario, it's the student who normally suffers, and at great expense. Thus each student looking for an instructor should check out his/her credentials very carefully.

Secondly, Braden said, oftentimes some intelligent instruction for young players is second-guessed by parents who intervene in the coach-student relationship.

Again, it's the student who suffers. The cure: The young student, the coach, and the parents need to be on the same page and that often requires carefully planned discussions and demonstrations.

Thirdly, children and adults who receive intelligent instruction are often resistant because change can be painful. Braden found tennis lessons can produce feelings quite similar to those experienced in therapy.

Thus, Braden continued, the job of an instructor is to help students feel comfortable while being uncomfortable. The job of the student is to expect some pain and to understand that it is a natural component when trying to change one's game.

Fourthly, Braden was surprised many times that students often fail to understand their responsibility that follows lessons. For example, a student might be making some significant gains during a lesson but will soon after sacrifice those gains in order to beat someone with their old strokes.

It goes something like this: "Right now I'll do anything to beat this person and I'll do what the coach wants next week."

Obviously, this system prolongs, or totally negates, one's chances to make major gains in the future, Braden pointed out. He believed that the term "practice makes perfect" needs to be revised to "intelligent practice improves one's chances of making the desired changes."

Practice has been studied over and over again, and the key is to practice in the same manner as one would be expected to perform in a match. Thus the cure is to treat every shot with respect it deserves and to attempt the new stroke, regardless of the outcome of the match.

Braden believed it would be in the best interests of all students to learn how to have fun while making meaningful changes. It simply means that one is willing to go through some pain in the present to have years and years of fun in the future.

How can you properly assess strengths and weaknesses? Braden's suggestions:

1. Make your own list of your strengths and weaknesses as you see them.
2. Ask your coach, or a coach who knows your game, to list them.
3. Ask players who compete against you on a regular basis how they would assess your game.

4. Set a video camera at the top of the court fence and in the center. Then play a match against someone stronger than yourself. Most cameras will play a minimum of sixty minutes and that will often cover two sets.

Play the tape and make notes when strengths and weaknesses appear. Look carefully at the components of each strength and weakness. This can be done by playing each stroke frame by frame. The reasons for successes and failures become obvious.

Research clearly indicates, Braden said, that intelligent practice must simulate actual playing conditions. However, before playing it's wise to review each stroke very slowly to make certain you are on the right track.

The word "slowly" is very important as one's brain and central nervous system can quickly record changes needed when the action is produced in a slow and methodical manner, according to Braden. Once those changes are recorded, the next step is to be able to reproduce them when competing.

Next, with the assistance of a friend work on drills that will produce the shots you are attempting to improve.

The final step is to see if you can introduce the changes in actual playing conditions. Video recording can be a great aid when assessing changes in one's game.

As Braden noted, researchers have shown that the most successful players are those who are "process-oriented." They are only concerned about hitting each shot properly and are not thinking about possible outcomes.

"One's brain has trouble sending down more than one electrical message to the muscles," Braden said. "If one is only concerned about proper stroke production, the outcome will take care of itself."

Winning with Character

In writing about character development in his book *The Only Way to Win*, Dr. Jim Loehr quoted champion Martina Navratilova as saying: "The moment of victory is much too short to live for that and nothing else." She should know because she experienced more victories than any female tennis player ever.

Loehr believes players should not spend energy on determining why it is they're doing what they're doing, because they have defined an ultimate purpose that holds up to scrutiny. "In fact, you will find it magnificently energizing when what you do—when everything you do—serves the purpose of helping you get ever closer to the ideal you have set for yourself," he says in his book.

Loehr points out that when we really want something, we invest our energy in greater quantity and with greater quality, focus, and intensity. "It is within our control to stop investing energy in things that are not fulfilling and begin investing in things that are. If, for example, you want to overcome narcissistic tendencies, you must build your capacity for compassion, humility, and gratitude by investing your energy directly in them. This is not to say that it's easy or that it happens quickly. It isn't and doesn't. But that is how change occurs: in response to an intentional change in the course of energy. As you purposely invest energy in this new character-centered way, you are training your 'inner coach.'"

Loehr writes about what players are told at the Orlando, Florida–based Human Performance Institute headquarters, which he helped found. They have a small elite tennis academy in which boys and girls between the ages of ten and eighteen train hard five days a week to become world-class players. On day one of their training, academy participants are told the following:

"At this academy, we use the demands and stress of elite tennis to most importantly help you become strong, resilient people of great character. We care about your tennis but we care more about who you are becoming because of tennis. Our most important imperative at this academy is winning with character. Every day represents another opportunity to grow in self-control, respect for others, persistence, positivity, and trustworthiness. No matter how far you go as a player, if you use tennis to strengthen character, tennis will always be a priceless gift."

Loehr says the simple act of re-purposing tennis to become a vehicle for accelerating character development gives meaning and value to all the years of training whether or not the goal to play professional tennis ever becomes realized. He believes that any achievement goal can be re-purposed to become an opportunity to grow strengths of character. Regardless of whether one succeeds or fails in that external achievement itself, something of real value will have been gained.

"Nice guys finish last, the saying goes in sport and is meant to apply to life in general," Loehr writes. "The corporate equivalent might be: Women and men of high character have more trouble reaching the top."

Loehr's experience at HPI tells him that's not true at all. "We look no further than the countless sport competitors we've had the good fortune to work with like Olympic speed skating champion Dan Jansen, Monica Seles, and Jim Courier, who display remarkable compassion, respect, and caring for others off the playing field and all became the best in the world in their sport," Loehr said. "The notion that to be a great competitor, one must be a callused, cold, and ruthless personality is a most unfortunate misrepresentation of the truth."

Loehr notes that HPI players are coached to use winning, losing, and the demands of tennis to become extraordinary people. He says they work very hard every day at tennis to become the people they want to be, to grow the muscles that will one day define their greatest assets.

"Our hope is that the pursuit of tennis in this special way will serve as a template for them throughout their lives, providing guidance in how and why to pursue anything and everything," he says. "The hope is that this will enable them to live lives of great value to the end, without regrets.

"So much of what the kids learn at the HPI Tennis Academy is filtered through what happens on the court. When they lose, they know they have more to learn. They also know that winning too much can arouse an exaggerated view of oneself, a sense of superiority, even an invincibility that is unrealistic and damaging. We want our players to be challenged seriously but still win more than half the time, if possible. When they lose, the internal learning is typically richer and deeper, each loss a chance to build resiliency, persistence, perspective, and dedication."

He adds, "Our student-athletes have a love affair with tennis—unlike, I'm sad to say, far too many children and teens in other elite junior training programs. Our kids love tennis because they see it for what it is—a fabulous opportunity to grow up and build physical, emotional, mental, and spiritual strength. So if they never make it to the top of professional tennis, they will still value all the hard work and sacrifices they have invested because, most importantly, it helped them build their inner core of life strengths."

Loehr's intimate, decades-long involvement in professional tennis has provided him with a long list of current and former professional tennis players who bust the myth that champions need to be jerks, that external success must somehow go hand in hand with character deficit: To mention just a few, he listed Kim Clijsters, winner of four Grand Slam titles; Bob and Mike Bryan, the greatest doubles team in tennis history; and Maria Sharapova, Monica Seles, Patrick Rafter, Todd Martin, and Tom and Tim Gullikson.

Enjoy Yourself and Succeed

It's very difficult to excel at something you don't enjoy, Murray says. To find greater enjoyment in tennis, he offers the following principles:

1. Challenge and success: Structure lessons and practice so that it fully challenges you, but so that success occurs more frequently than failure. This increases perceived competence and motivation.
2. Reward proper performance: This includes good effort, sportsmanship, and proper use of mental skills.
3. Frequent praise: Praise yourself and others both verbally and non-verbally.

4. Novelty: Keep learning interesting by varying the routine often.
5. Socially connected: Let others help you in making important decisions, and seek frequent feedback from others about your progress.
6. Realistic goals: Make sure your goals are not set too high or too low. Focus primarily on performance goals rather than outcome goals.
7. Have fun! Every day seek new ways to make tennis fun.

Braden pointed out that in our society, the measure of tennis success is normally one's ranking in competitive play. "How sad that we often place the emphasis in the wrong place," he said. "The most accepted goal for coaches is to help each person maximize performance and enjoyment of our great game in the shortest period of time. It would pay each of us to re-read this goal from time to time. In addition to the coaches, that advice also goes out to parents and children."

Seldom does one hear the losers talk about their joy of even being invited to an event, Braden noted. Yet there are thousands of young players who would like to have been invited and weren't.

The sport of tennis has opportunities that you see in no other sport. One can play as an individual, or as a team. One can play for eight or nine decades. The physical and mental health benefits are legendary.

ACKNOWLEDGMENTS

With deep appreciation, the author acknowledges the support and guidance of the following people who helped make this book possible:

- Lorenzo Beltrame: The Director of Athletic Performance Coaching and Director of Tennis at the Johnson & Johnson Human Performance Institute in Orlando, Florida.
- Dr. Richard Berger, MD, an orthopedic surgeon at the Mayo Clinic in Rochester, Minnesota, who has performed surgery on several top pro tennis players.
- Sly Black Tennis Academy, Boca Raton, Florida: Thanks for providing the facility and players to pose for the photographs in this book.
- Nick Bollettieri: Legendary tennis coach, author, the founder of the IMG/Bollettieri Academy in Bradenton, Florida, and an inductee into the International Tennis Hall of Fame.
- Wayne Bryan: A teaching pro for more than thirty years in Southern California, father of Bob and Mike, the best men's doubles team in pro tennis history, author of the book *Raising Your Child to Be a Champion in Athletics, Arts, and Academics*. Also lecturer and motivational speaker.
- Jeff Drock MS, CSCS: A Certified Strength and Conditioning Specialist based in Florida who works with world-ranked junior, college, and professional players and is a contributing writer for several publications. Special thanks to Jeff for writing the instructional exercises that accompany the photographs in this book.
- Pat Etcheberry: A legend in the field of sports fitness and movement who has coached hundreds of champion athletes including Pete Sampras, Justine Henin, and Andre Agassi. He is based at Mission Inn Resort & Club in Howey-in-the-Hills, Florida.

- Allen Fox, Ph.D.: An acclaimed California-based tennis coach, sports psychologist, and author of several books including *The Winner's Mind*.
- Chuck Gately: A teaching pro of players at all levels in New England and Florida for forty-five years, US Professional Tennis Association member, founder of Ivy League of Tennis Camps in New England, and founder the Lads and Lassie International Junior Tournament in Florida.
- Jonathan Hersch, MD: An orthopedic surgeon in the Miami, Florida, area specializing in sports medicine.
- Chris Jordan: The Director of Exercise Physiology at the Johnson & Johnson Human Performance Institute in Orlando, Florida.
- Michele Krause: The Tennis Industry Association's Cardio Tennis Manager. She co-founded Cardio Tennis ten years ago and today there are 1.5 million participants in the United States and it is offered in thirty countries.
- Bob Larson: Long-time tennis journalist and founder-publisher of Bob Larson's Daily Tennis.
- Jim Loehr, Ph.D.: A world-renowned performance psychologist and co-founder of the Johnson & Johnson Human Performance Institute in Orlando and author of fifteen books.
- Rick Macci: Internationally acclaimed coach based in Boca Raton, Florida, who trained five players in their formative years who became number 1 in the world—Jennifer Capriati, Andy Roddick, Venus Williams, Serena Williams, and Maria Sharapova—and is the author of *Macci Magic: Extracting Greatness from Yourself and Others*.
- Al Messerschmidt: A Florida-based photographer specializing in sports and travel. For forty years he has covered major events including Super Bowls, tennis and golf US Opens, horse racing, NASCAR, boxing, the NBA, NHL,

and MLS. Messerschmidt's photo archive includes more than a million images dating to the 1930s.

- John F. Murray, Ph.D.: A licensed clinical and sports psychologist in Palm Beach, Florida, who works with a variety of amateur, junior, Olympic, and professional athletes, including tennis players and NFL teams. He has written two books: *Smart Tennis: How to play and Win the Mental Game* and *The Mental Performance Index.*
- Bill Norris: For more than forty years on the men's circuit, he treated everyone from Rod Laver to Jimmy Connors to John McEnroe to Roger Federer and Rafael Nadal. He wrote *Pain, Set and Match* with journalist Richard Evans and now runs a consultancy in Boca Raton, Florida, treating young and old.
- Satoshi Ochi: Head Strength and Conditioning Coach for the USTA's High Performance training center in Boca Raton, Florida.
- Robert S. Weinberg, Ph.D.: A professor of physical education, health, and sports studies at Miami University in Ohio and an internationally respected author and past president of the Association for the Advancement of Applied Sports Psychology.

ABOUT THE AUTHOR

Photo by Alese Pechter

Jim Martz is the publisher-editor of *Florida Tennis Magazine*, which he founded in 1992. He also is editor of CaneSport.com, an online publication that is the foremost authority of University of Miami sports.

He has written eight books, including *Tales from the Miami Hurricanes Sideline*, and has edited two books on tennis. He also has written numerous articles on tennis, college football, and soccer for several national publications.

Martz won the United States Tennis Association's Media Excellence Award for print in 2000 and was vice president of the US Tennis Writers Association.

Prior to launching Florida Tennis, he was a sports writer and editor for the Miami Herald and Des Moines Register, and he was a winner of the Iowa Associated Press News Writing Contest in sports.

He holds a B.A. in English from Alma College and a M.A. in mass communications from the University of Iowa. Born and raised in South Bend, Indiana, he resides in Florida.